Leonard Ottone was born in Italy before moving to Australia with his family as a young boy in the 1960s.

Growing up in a family of 10 children in Melbourne's northern suburbs and struggling at school, he turned to the streets where he was introduced to drugs and gained an education in crime.

In and out of juvenile detention as a youth, Leonard graduated to prison as a young man and eventually ended up in Pentridge where he continued to access drugs and maintain his habit. With the help of the other prisoners, Leonard finally learned to read and write as he struggled to write letters home to his family.

After many failed attempts, Leonard is recovering from his addiction and has established himself as an outreach professional, supporting others who struggle with addiction and successfully helping them to transform their lives.

He is the founder and CEO of Vicdor, a not-for-profit organisation that provides support and services to people struggling to overcome substance abuse.

leonardottone.com

COMING CLEAN

ONE MAN'S STRUGGLE TO OVERCOME A LIFE OF ADDICTION AND CRIME

LEONARD OTTONE

REAL
FILM AND PUBLISHING

First published in 2017
by Real Film and Publishing
www.realfp.com.au

Text copyright © Leonard Ottone 2017

The moral rights of the author have been asserted.

All rights reserved. No part of this publication may be reproduced, stored in a retrieval system or transmitted in any form by any means, electronic, mechanical, photocopying, recording or otherwise without the prior written permission of the author. Enquiries should be made to the publisher.

Cataloguing-in-Publication data is available from the National Library of Australia

Coming Clean

ISBN 978-0-9875179-9-9

Edited by Romy Moshinsky and Georgie Raik-Allen
Cover design and book design by Lisa Lipshut
Headshot © Kate Ballis

Disclaimer: many of the names used in this book have been changed in order to protect the identities of those characters and for legal reasons. Furthermore, some of the details have been modified, also for legal reasons.

To my children.
This is for you.

COMING CLEAN - CONTENTS

Foreword	8
Introduction	11
Part One - Childhood	**13**
Potenza	14
Carlton	16
North Roys	22
Trouble	24
Part Two - Delinquency	**30**
Turana	31
Shame	37
In the System	38
Coburg Bowls	41
Out of Control	43
Denise	45
First Hit	46
Americano	49
Charged with Rape	51
Part Three - Prison	**54**
Courier	55
Armed Robbery	56
Pentridge	59
Using Inside	63
Killing Time	66
Serving a Sentence	68
Karen & Chantelle	70
Breach of Parole	73
Won Wron Open Camp	78
Reality Hits	82
Red Alert	87
The Ride to H Division	90
60 Days	92
Getting Out	96
Part Four - Hung Out To Dry	**102**
Pistol & Possession Charges	103
Odyssey House	105
Relegated	110
No Hoper	115
Part Five - Recovery	**122**
Pleasant View	123
Us Society	128
Meeting Sue	131
Interviews	134
Working Life	137
Part Six - Waking The Monster	**140**
Injury	141
Becoming a Father Again	143
St Kilda Streets	145
My Fourth Child	148
Believing the Bullshit	149
Red Carpet	152
Burnt Out	154
Naomi	158
Farm Life	161
Giovanni Ottone	164
Italy	166
Tiyla	168
The Wedding	170
Part Seven - Relapse	**171**
The Honeymoon is Over	172
Chaos	174
Denial	178
Catch Me if You Can	180
April Fool	183
Bailed	186
The Trial	190
Part Eight - Moving On	**192**
Fresh Start	193
Vicdor	198
Travel	200
Home	203
Epilogue	216
Acknowledgements	220

FOREWORD

I met Leonard Ottone in the early 1990s. A handsome young man with a gentle demeanour and a vulnerability that I immediately connected to.

At the time I was volunteering with the Lighthouse Foundation where I was hearing horrific stories of abuse and neglect of young people, by their own families and through the system.

Leonard was working at the Lighthouse Foundation and I had no idea about his criminal history or his drug addiction until we both attended a self-development workshop, which gave me some understanding of his years of hiding his fears and inadequacies.

Peter and I have a farm on the Mornington Peninsula that we are slowly turning into a wildlife sanctuary. It had brought peace to my own life so I believed it could bring a moment of respite to the lives of people who had little space to breathe.

Leonard was running a support program for young people with significant problems, so I asked if he would be interested in bringing young people to the farm for a day or two. We would give them a little work in exchange for some peace and time out from the real world.

In later years, Leonard came to work for us part time and continued to bring young people with him to the farm. During that time he had a couple of relapses. I had learned enough at Lighthouse to have some understanding of addiction and personal trauma so we were able to look past the behaviour and see only his terrible pain. Knowing the real Leonard, it was easy to support a

FOREWORD

man whose only real need was to feel valued and loved.

Leonard continued to work for us for a number of years until one day I found him in the cottage at Flinders in a very bad state. He opened up to me about his relapse and I had no other option than to let him go and tell him that he could not come back until he was clean again. The next we heard, he'd been picked up by the police and charged with various drug-related offences. Most of these charges were later dropped and Leonard started on his road to recovery.

Leonard was extremely good at counselling young addicts. Because of his own history he knew exactly what they were thinking so they couldn't get away with anything. There are many people who owe their lives to him.

I have had personal experience of Leonard's power to help young people. My youngest daughter used drugs for a number of years. She was at Flinders for her birthday when she met Leonard and he asked her to go to a Narcotics Anonymous meeting with him. She was reluctant but decided to go. While there she heard a young man say, "I don't want to be cool anymore. Cool's too close to cold. I wanna be warm!" This had a profound effect on her. She immediately disposed of all her drug paraphernalia and never looked back. My daughter has now been drug free for 13 years. For this I will be forever grateful that Leonard is my friend.

For years Leonard would tell me that he would like to write his story. I tried to encourage him but it never eventuated. Then I heard about a writer and publisher called Romy Moshinsky who could work with Leonard and facilitate the writing process.

I told Leonard how important it was for his children and his

COMING CLEAN

family to understand what had happened in his life to cause such chaos. I told him how much it would help other addicts if they knew it was possible to turn their own lives around, as well as teenagers who might not be seduced into using drugs if they knew where it could lead. I told him how proud he should be of what he had achieved and how much I admired his strength and courage in sharing his story.

Leonard is a kind and loyal man with a huge heart and I would trust him with my life. I am proud to have him as a friend.

Vicki Vidor OAM

INTRODUCTION

I used to give talks to parents of addicts. I would tell my story - and many would ask if there was a book about my life. So I started to write.

For many years, I tried to sit and write about my life but that involved confronting my past, which has never been easy for me. The events in this book include experiences I've been continuously trying to run away from.

I have been in and out of recovery since 1989. And for over a decade, I've let go of everything to do with crime and drugs. I am seen as a guy who helps kids addicted to drugs - a guru - and when young people look up to you, they don't want to hear that you are struggling. That fear of revealing my vulnerability to people who depend on my strength hindered the progress of this book. I also worried about the hurt that I would cause if I brought up events that people had dealt with and moved on from.

The other problem that dogged me was my struggle with reading and writing. Until I was in my twenties I was essentially illiterate. Writing a book is a difficult and slow process for someone whose basic skills were learned in Pentridge Prison from other prisoners while they helped me write letters home.

My life, the shit I have done, the events I was trying to write about - they are not stories that are easily shared with my six children. There are plenty of experiences from my past I would prefer to deny. But my kids have questions. They are seeking to understand me better, to understand their history and in turn, to

COMING CLEAN

better know themselves. It's time to come clean to Chantelle, Teryn, Dean, Michaela, Jake and Tiyla.

All my fears about exposing my history had to be weighed against giving hope – letting people know there is life after drugs and crime. It is possible to leave your past behind, repair your relationships and contribute to society in a positive and healthy way.

I am ready to hang it out there, to admit to everything. I have no secrets.

Leonard Ottone

PART ONE – CHILDHOOD
1959 – 1973

POTENZA

I was born in a barn in a small village near Naples called Potenza. It was 1959 and life in southern Italy was tough.

I was the third child born into a family that would grow rapidly until I was one of 10 siblings competing for the love and attention of our parents.

My parents, Rosa and Giovanni, had married in my mother's home town of Corleto, perched on the top of a hill and overlooking the beautiful countryside.

The barn, our home, was no more than a chook pen; my mum and dad slept in a made-up bed on the floor while my siblings and I slept in hammocks hanging from hooks in the rafters.

My parents named me after my father's mother, Leonarda but my mum didn't like her mother-in-law so she always called me Dino or Dean, a name that some of my brothers and sisters still use today. I only learned that my real name was Leonard when my first set of criminal charges were read out in court many years later.

There was a lot of superstitious talk in the village about an elderly woman who was putting curses on children. One day she came to our little home and as soon as she left I became violently ill. I continued to be a sickly child and my mother was convinced that I had been cursed.

According to my mum, I had a horrific early childhood. My dad would tie me to the cot and leave me there for hours on end so that I wouldn't wander away while he worked in the paddocks. My mum always believed there was a connection between me being locked up as a young child and the years I spent as an adult locked in prison.

My parents grew much of our own food and made everything we needed by hand: sausages, wine, even soap out of lard. My dad was a hard worker. In Italy he worked the land, turning the ground in paddocks. But he was also a drinker and a womaniser. He would leave my mother for months at a time, then return home and get her pregnant again, before taking off once more in search of more work and drink.

My mother was tiny, beautiful and fragile-looking but she was in fact very strong, strong enough to raise our family almost single-handedly.

CARLTON

In 1961 my father decided to go to Australia where he believed we would have more opportunities and the chance to escape the hardships of life in Italy. So off he went, leaving my mum with four young children. God bless her soul.

When Dad arrived in Melbourne he stayed with friends and distant family and worked as a labourer, digging trenches and laying sewerage pipes in new suburbs. He worked seven days a week, eight to 12 hours a day for two years, saving any money he could. To relax he spent time with the local Italian community in the cafes in Lygon Street or drinking at the pub.

At the end of 1962, Dad flew back to see us in Italy for a few months. Then he left again, leaving my mother pregnant with her fifth child.

Eventually, we followed him back to Australia on the ship, the *SS Roma*. My mother and her children - Giuseppe (Joe) aged eight, Antionetta (Annette), six, myself aged four, Rocco, two, and Carmella (Carmel) just five months old. I remember the cabins were small and that I got into trouble a lot. We were trying to run around and it was difficult for Mum to contain four small children while caring for a baby.

Arriving in Port Melbourne on 24 February 1964 was a huge deal. We were greeted by cousins we had never met and of course my father who I didn't really remember. They were all picking me up and hugging and kissing me. I can recall cameras and streamers and lots of noise. There was a feast to celebrate our arrival with every type of Italian food you can imagine: antipasto, pasta, meat, cheeses and all sorts of wine – red, white and grappa.

We moved into a two-bedroom house in Rathdowne Street, Carlton. I slept with three siblings in one room and Mum and Dad slept with Carmella in the other room. Dad continued working and I started going to childcare, although I didn't speak any English and I had no idea what was going on.

A year later we moved to Lee St, Carlton. We always lived in an Italian area and my dad worked with Italians and would never learn to speak English. My mum stayed home. I started prep at Lee Street Primary School, a very small school just 20 metres away from home. I was the Italian kid with no English and I remember even then feeling that I didn't fit in. To make things worse I was always wearing hand-me-downs while my younger brother (who was nearly the same size as me) was given new clothes. Mum had her sixth child during that time. Salvatore (Sam) was born on 7 January 1965.

Not long after we moved into a two-bedroom terrace in Rae Street, North Fitzroy - the first house my parents ever bought. It had a small study that became a third bedroom, so we went from sleeping in hammocks that hung from the roof in Italy to squeezing into a couple of bedrooms full of mattresses. I moved schools to attend Alfred Crescent Primary School which was also a close walk from home.

My memories kick in from about this age. Each morning I would set off to school with my older brother and sister, while Mum stayed home to look after the younger ones and my dad went to work. After work he would come home, throw his bag over the front fence, and go straight to the Tramway Hotel directly across the road.

Sometimes Dad would come home from the pub for dinner and other times he would return very late, screaming and aggressive. My dad was often very drunk and always intimidating, and I'm sure everyone else in the family was as terrified of him as I was. I never saw him hit my mum but I copped a lot. A kick up the arse or a swipe to the side of the head was his form of discipline, his way of getting us to come to the dinner table quickly or go to bed without complaint.

Mum decided to move us to St Bridges Catholic Primary School when I was in grade three. By then I was speaking English but my reading and writing was not very good. The teachers gave me a lot of leeway because I came from Italy. In hindsight, they gave me too much leeway.

I pretended to be really naughty and used that as an excuse not to do my homework. But the truth was there was no one at home to help me and I was really struggling. I didn't want anyone to know that I couldn't read or write.

I remember my mum preparing me round loaves of bread with thick salami for my lunch. I was embarrassed and ate my 'foreign' food on the way to school so no one would see. My older brother and sister seemed to settle better than me, they made their own friends and I often felt like the annoying younger brother always tagging along.

By this stage Maria and Dominic had been born. I was eight years old and already starting to disconnect from the family. I would wake up in the morning and leave the house as quickly as possible – either getting to school very early or going to my friend Ray's house directly over the road from school. His mum and dad would leave for work and we would watch TV or kick a football before the bell rang.

I started hanging around with a few other boys who liked to play football or soccer at recess and lunchtime. Returning home to our small house at the end of the day was always intense. My dad was often drunk and I started fighting with my brothers and sisters.

By the time I was 10 or 11, my behaviour started to worry my mum, my elder brother Joe and a couple of teachers. I was wagging school, shoplifting from milk bars and doing anything to avoid going home.

On one of the days I was playing truant, the priest at St Bridges found my bag in my locker and decided to bring it home. He wasn't trying to get me in trouble, he was genuinely concerned about my welfare. That was the first time I had my parent's undivided attention; I felt acknowledged, it was a lightbulb moment for me. Dad was furious but I couldn't get into too much trouble because the priest was there. He warned me in Italian, "*Ti racomondo*", it's village slang, roughly meaning, "I recommend to you" or "I'm warning you!" That was my quality time with my mum and dad.

One afternoon I ran off with a couple of friends, Ray and John. We left school and went down to Merri Creek, just mucking around and avoiding going home. It started to get dark and we got lost in the drains and ended up miles away. I started to panic but eventually we were picked up by the police and taken home. By then I was even more scared of the trouble I was going to get into with my dad and prayed that he was still drinking at the pub.

COMING CLEAN

My mum had been very worried; she threatened to tell my dad and sent me to bed where I lay awake anticipating what would happen when my father came home. I could barely breathe. Eventually I fell asleep but the next morning Mum again threatened to tell Dad when he got home and I spent the day riddled with fear.

I spent many days worrying about what was going to happen, or wishing something would happen so I could get past it. My dad was a very happy drunk when we had visitors but other times he turned into an angry, overbearing brute who terrified me. I couldn't understand why this fear wasn't enough to stop me from behaving the way I did. Perhaps any type of attention from him – no matter how frightening – was better than none at all.

One day in my final year of primary school I stayed back after the bell, kicking the footy with friends. Someone came up with the idea of breaking into our classroom so, trying to impress everyone, I climbed the outside wall using the heavy steel pipes bolted to the wall as footholds. Once I got inside, I went downstairs and let in the others. In our classroom we found the boxes where students put money for swearing, being late and other minor offences. So we split the money between the four of us and, thinking we'd had a great adventure, took off home.

The next morning we were called, one by one, to the principal's office to face the consequences. We were all given the strap and then made to stand in the playground with our faces looking at the brick wall; we weren't allowed to talk to anyone and had to stand there for most of the day. It was so shameful, being put on show like that, and I was terrified that my parents would find out.

In our family, my elder brother Joe was the good boy, he went to school and worked part time. My big sister helped Mum in the home, and all the younger kids went through their own kind of hell I suppose. But I was the one who started getting into trouble at school and eventually with the police. Staring at bricks was something I would do a lot more of in the years ahead.

NORTH ROYS

I started playing basketball with a team called North Roys while at St Bridges. It was a blessing for me; I loved the weekly training, Friday night games, and competing in tournaments throughout the state. It was the best part of my life because I felt like I was finally part of something.

Most of my teammates were school friends; Gezza was our captain, and Ray, Paul and I were the main players. Every Friday night one of the other parents would drive us to the game, usually at the main stadium in Albert Park. One of the senior coaches, Vince, drove a Valiant Hemi Pacer so we would all try to get a lift with him.

The early days when we were still learning were a bit tough and we got flogged in most of our under 11s games. I can still remember the feeling the first time we finally won a game – we were ecstatic. The team gradually improved while we played in the under 12s and under 13s, until we graduated to the A grade competition in the under 14s.

My parents gave me enough money to cover the fees but, unlike the other kids, I never had any money for snacks and drinks after the match. One day, while subbed off during a game, a wallet fell out of some clothes as I moved them aside to sit down. Before I had a chance to think about what I was doing, I picked up the wallet and put it in my bag.

The coach put me back on court but I couldn't concentrate; I just wanted the game to be over so I could see what was in the wallet. After the game I went to the change rooms and was rapt to find $70 and some change. Telling no one, I threw the wallet in the bin and bought myself a drink and a hotdog; finally I knew what it felt like to have some spending money.

After that, every time I played basketball I would try to go through bags and jeans while sitting on the bench, looking for more money to steal. I figured everyone else was better off than me and I deserved my share. One night we were told to be careful with our belongings and not to leave money or valuables lying around as people had been reporting thefts.

Then one Friday night a couple of detectives turned up at the stadium looking for me. The North Roys were playing on the back court so the two huge men in suits walked through 11 other courts to tell me that I needed to accompany them to the police station to answer some questions.

As it turned out, the questions were related to other petty crimes, not the thefts at the stadium. But my team mates knew I was in trouble with the police and I can still remember the shame of being paraded out by the cops.

After that, my days of playing with the team were numbered. My criminal activity was catching up with me. I lost my connection with basketball – the one thing in my life I seemed to be good at and that gave me a sense of belonging.

TROUBLE

By 1972, I had nine siblings including Italo and Roberto. I was 12 years old and it was time for me to start high school at Collingwood Technical College. It was a huge school in a rough area and I woke up every day full of fear.

After breakfast – usually bread and warm milk – I walked to school with my older brother who was already in form three (year nine). I felt okay walking to school with him; people would yell out, "Hey Joe, what's happening?" and somehow that alone would make me feel important.

However once we got to school the crippling fear returned. Collingwood Tech was a very strict all boys' school. I knew I didn't belong there, that I should be back in primary school learning to read and write. I was completely out of my league.

After a while I became friendly with Chris and Ron who were both a little older than me. It didn't take much for them to convince me to start wagging school with them. We would go to class to get our names marked off the roll and then as soon as possible (sometimes we would have to wait till lunch time) we would sneak away to hang out in Smith Street or look for a house to break into.

Usually, I was told to keep watch while Chris and Ron broke into the house, and to whistle if it looked like the police or the owners were showing up. When they came out we would walk off like nothing had happened. Once we cleared the area we would start talking about what Chris and Ron had stolen – money, jewellery, other knickknacks – and we'd split it three ways. The problem with standing guard was that I never knew what they had pocketed before the split.

Then we'd usually head into the city to spend the stolen money on new clothes or to do some shoplifting. Myer was a favourite; we'd steal things like clothes and stationary. At times we'd shoplift things that weren't even worth the risk just as a dare.

Of course, I couldn't go home with new clothes so I'd leave them in my locker and in the mornings before school I would take off my brother's hand-me-downs - which I hated - and put on my new clothes.

For the first time in my life, I started to feel some confidence; I had money in my pocket, cool clothes and a couple of friends who trusted me. It seemed easier to wag school and burgle houses than to talk to anyone about the difficulties I was having with reading and writing. I kept my fear of school to myself.

Never once did I think about the upset we were causing other people through our criminal activity. I had never owned anything of value myself so I didn't know what it would feel like to have something taken away. I felt that getting my hands on those stolen goods was my right.

Then one day we got caught. The store security called the police and the drama began: first the questioning, then the charges - back then it was called larceny - then calling our parents. We didn't have a phone at home, and neither Mum or Dad could speak a word of English so for a while I got away with translating, minimising the actual charges and telling them I was just with other kids who had been caught stealing. I was given a good behaviour bond and told that if I stayed out of trouble the charges would be forgotten.

In reality I was crying out for help, but all anyone noticed was loud, inappropriate behaviour, and I was treated accordingly - like a delinquent teenager. I was playing truant from school more often than attending, I did no homework and was basically illiterate - something I didn't admit to anyone.

Gradually my criminal activity stepped up; from lookout duty I graduated to breaking into houses myself, I shoplifted anything that wasn't pinned down and started stealing cars to take on joy rides. Most times we got away with it but occasionally we got caught. Life started to get a little hectic.

At home, Dad was working hard to support our huge family of 10 children while Mum was inundated with feeding and clothing the kids and trying to run the household. My siblings appeared to be going okay, but who really knew. Meanwhile I was on a 12-month good behaviour bond with the Melbourne Children's Court.

Everything was continuing as before, only now I was finally attracting some sort of attention. I was creating an interesting identity for myself; I was no longer invisible.

Joe, me, Annette and Rocco (front).
Italy, 1963

Before departing Italy for
Melbourne. 1964

Back row: Me, Annette, Joe
Front row: Carmen, Sam, Rocco. 1970

Sunday lunch at home in Rae Street, North Fitzroy. 1970

With my family at Italo's baptism. 1971

Me, Carmen, Rocco, Annette, Joe and Sam. Carmen's confirmation. 1972

With my younger brothers Dom (back) and Italo. Before becoming a state ward. 1974

PART TWO – DELINQUENCY
1974 – 1977

TURANA

In January 1974, my offending caught up with me and I was sentenced and made a ward of the state; I was sent to Turana, the youth justice centre in Park Street, Parkville. I had no idea how long I was going to be there.

I had just turned 14 but felt young compared to some of the guys living there: tattooed, hardened crims with reputations, fighters. I was only a petty thief. I acted like I was coping but the whole time I was shit scared. The routine was: wake up, eat breakfast, sit around most of the time. Some of the older guys looked after me, told me I could chill with them. But deep down I knew I wasn't in their league (and mistakenly thought I never would be).

At first the only people who visited me were counsellors. I didn't get a single letter from anyone in my family and there was no phone at home so I couldn't even call. Finally, after several weeks, my family started coming to see me. It was clear that things at home weren't going too well. Dad was still drinking and Mum was stressed about her parents in Italy who were unwell. Having a son confined in Turana added to her worries.

After a couple of months I was finally released to an outpatient program in Brunswick where I was kept under supervision and told to attend group counselling sessions while living back at home.

My family moved from Fitzroy to a much bigger house with four huge bedrooms in Coburg East. Soon after, my mum went to Italy for four months with my eldest brother Joe and my youngest brother Robert. I was really angry with my mum. Why didn't she take me? I was the one getting in trouble; I was the one who needed a break from reality. Feeling abandoned and unloved, I started wagging school again.

Most mornings I'd leave the house to go to school, meet up with a couple of mates and our day would begin - cruising the streets, looking for a house to break into. We were smoking dope, doing burglaries, shoplifting. We would break into a factory and steal weird stuff like chairs and a coffee table. I would take them home in a taxi and tell my dad that I'd made them at school.

While Mum, Joe and Robert were away, my sister Annette was meant to help out more at home. Instead, she took off. For a week, we didn't hear from her. We then found out that she had got herself locked up in Winlaton, a female youth training centre. She was made a ward of the state for three weeks. For a while, the focus was off me.

When my mum and brothers finally came back from Italy after four long months, everyone seemed happy to have them back, but I could tell that Dad resented Mum for having left him to work like a dog and take care of eight kids by himself.

Life seemed to settle for a while but before long I caused another headache for myself and everyone else. One day, my mates and I broke into and ransacked a house in North Fitzroy. We found some cash and split it four ways, but some in the group were not satisfied and so we decided to do another burglary. We broke into a small terrace house in Fitzroy, ransacking bedrooms and looking for money and jewellery. We were all pretty stoned and feeling good; but not for long. After we left, we were walking along Rae Street when two cars pulled up on either side of us and screeched to a halt. Doors swung open and huge men emerged with their guns drawn. "Stop, hands up… against the wall."

We were caught off guard and none of us had a chance to take off. Once we had been searched and the money and other items found, we were handcuffed and made to sit on the curb. We were separated, told not to speak to each other and questioned. Soon a divvy van arrived and two of us were thrown in the back, the door slammed behind us – the noise of the lock echoed in my ear. I looked back through the rear window and could see the other two were separated into two more vans. The ride to the Fitzroy police station only took about 10 minutes, but it felt like hours; every time the van turned a corner we were thrown from one side to the other; every time it braked, we were thrown backwards.

At the station we were taken into separate rooms. I was immobilised with fear; the detectives were fucking huge and I didn't know what to say or do. When you get caught coming out of a house that's not yours, you can't actually say, "I don't know what you're talking about," so I admitted to that burglary and a couple of others (although, not knowing what the others were saying, I told the police that I couldn't remember the location of the other houses we'd burgled).

The cops found out between all the different interviews that we had been involved in a particular burglary where some rifles had been stolen and they made it clear they wanted the rifles returned. One of my mates, Chris had taken the guns and only he knew where they were.

While we were all in the same room being fingerprinted, the cops told us that bail would not be offered until the guns were returned. The biggest cop asked Chris where the guns were and as Chris attempted to say he didn't know, he was hit on the nose so hard that I heard a crack and saw blood pouring from his mouth and nose. The cop said that if blood hit the floor Chris would have to lick it up, so he pulled his jumper out in front of him to try and mop up all the blood. By this stage I was shitting myself.

Chris revealed the location of the guns and the police retrieved them from under the floorboards of an empty house. Finally, we were all bailed. Because of my age, I was going to be taken home - fuck! I was given the charges and bail papers, and, with fingerprint ink still on some of my fingers, I was put in the back of a divvy van to be driven home. Thoughts raced through my head: what was going to happen, was my dad going to be home, how drunk would he be. I wished we would have an accident on the way. I couldn't cry; I just prayed silently. Please god help me; please god don't let him hurt me; please god; please god.

They pulled up outside my parents' place at about six o'clock, dinner time. The cops came around the back of the van, opened it up. I should have run there and then. My elder brother Joe opened the door and talked to the police; I hoped he'd lie and cover for me but my dad came to the front door with my mum behind him and brothers and sisters filling the hallway. It was not the best way to gain my family's attention.

Although he didn't speak any English, my father was able to thank the police and say goodbye. The sound of the cops walking away, the door closing behind me, and my family running back to their positions around the table, sent a shiver down my spine.

My dad turned to me and said in Italian, "Is this what they teach you at school?" He pushed me into his bedroom, walked in behind me and my very bad day got much worse.

Dad was a big man with huge hands; he hit me first with an open hand until I hit the ground. The hits turned to kicks that turned into whacks with the belt. I was hunched over in the corner trying to stop the blows; my screams and crying were muffled from the blood in my mouth and nose. My family was on the other side of the locked door trying to get in while my dad yelled abuse: "You piece of shit, you should be ashamed of yourself. This is what you're doing while I'm working like a dog to put food on the table? Fucking bastard. Piece of shit." It seemed to go on forever.

Finally Dad opened the door and Joe came in, followed by my mum who was in tears. I tried to get behind my brother for some form of protection but it didn't work, he turned around and hit me himself like a fucking coward. Once again I heard the noise of footsteps as my family ran back down the hallway to their seats at the table. I tried to contain the blood in my mouth and nose as, for the second time that day, I heard the threat: if blood hits the table I will really give you something to cry about.

I clearly remember looking at my dad at the other end of the table, my brothers and sisters to the left and right of me, my mother with tears in her eyes. If she said anything, she would be next to get the blame from dad: what sort of mother are you? Eyes stared at me while I tried to eat a bowl of spaghetti with tears and blood pouring down my face.

My father finally had enough of me and sent me to my room; the relief was indescribable. I had felt like a freak, beaten like that then made to sit in front of everyone, stared at like a side show, like a showpiece - an example of what happens when you get brought home by the police.

I walked into my room and sat down on the bed facing the mirror and truly broke down. I cried quietly for a while until l finally looked up. For another few minutes, I looked in the mirror, wondering whether, if I looked hard enough, I might see what was wrong with me. l didn't see a piece of shit or a criminal; I saw a 14-year-old who was lost, confused, beaten, shamed, fearful. I wiped the dry blood from my face, undressed and got into bed, praying no one would come in to talk to me. Finally, I fell asleep in the foetal position.

SHAME

Waking up, I was flooded with shame. Knowing Dad wasn't home was a relief but I still had to face the rest of the family.

I put on my game face - it was something I had learnt to do to survive; there were no good mornings in my house. Grunts, murmurs and looks from my siblings that could kill or that were filled with pity. Washed, dressed and caught a tram from Bell Street all the way to Johnston Street, Fitzroy and then walked to the tech school.

Two of the other kids that had been charged didn't show up at school but Chris was there and was already talking about getting smarter at committing crimes. That took me by surprise - he was either a fucking idiot or one cool customer.

School was just a place to go, I wasn't learning anything, just going through the motions. While the heat was on, I tried to be on my best behaviour but that wore thin and soon enough I started wagging and getting into trouble again.

It wasn't too long before the charges were heard and l was sent back to Turana. Back in the welfare system where more of the same would be further ingrained in me, and thousands of others. I went straight into a section called Class B, where younger kids were sent before being moved to either a minimal, medium or maximum section, depending on security status and level of crime.

IN THE SYSTEM

The time went by, day by day. I was getting used to life in the welfare system. There was structure and a schedule that suited me. There were no expectations of me; no one to disappoint. Before I knew it, the boys I had met became associates to hang out with, or to work with in the kitchen or laundry. They were all as fucked up as me so I was comfortable in their presence.

Drugs and self-abuse at Turana were a part of the culture. One day I walked into the bathroom and saw a guy who was dry retching and vomiting blood; drinking metho over a period of time had ripped the guts out of him. Despite these obvious warnings, as a young man, I didn't really understand the consequences of using and honestly believed my crimes had nothing to do with popping pills, smoking dope or drinking piss, so I just continued to take whatever I could lay my hands on.

Many of the younger boys looked up to the serial offenders, respected them for their crimes, and their on-the-edge lifestyles. I was in awe of some of these guys, they appeared to walk around so sure of themselves, fearless and charismatic. At times I wondered if they felt like me - outwardly okay but deep down riddled with self-doubt. I was filled with fear but acting with arrogance. I was right to be scared; many of the boys I was incarcerated with grew up to be notorious in the criminal underworld.

I was lucky to share a room with Dan. He was my age but was already a hardened criminal. He had my back and I was never picked on; others weren't so fortunate. It also worked to my advantage that

IN THE SYSTEM

I was quiet and kind of irrelevant.

Visiting days were interesting. Mum, Dad and occasionally a brother or two, would visit. After about five minutes, there was never much left to say. Dad would sit there looking at me with contempt; Mum would worry about how I was eating and when I was coming home; my younger siblings were intrigued by the whole experience, they'd look around, take it all in. During the visits, it seemed that the attention was all mine, undivided. It was all about me and I thrived on it; finally my five minutes of fame.

After the visits, I would return to a life that I was becoming comfortable with; the discipline and routine of the institution kept me occupied. Worrying about fitting in out there in the big world was consuming but still, I couldn't wait to get out.

Back then I was considered a first-timer with medium to minimal level security requirements but after a few months I was sent to Blue Gables, an open section for inmates getting ready for release, including older boys who had serious criminal backgrounds. It was a place where you learn quickly to keep your mouth shut and not be a smart arse.

Finally, the state released me back home, again under the supervision of the Brunswick Unit (later known as the Brosnan Centre), a halfway house for young men released from youth detention centres.

I attended twice a week and reported to a worker who was supervising my order. Theoretically, the unit played a valuable role in the community, however it was detrimental to my chances of rehabilitation as the guys I mixed with there had been in and out of the system all their lives. They were hardened, skilled and, at times, desperate crims who could steal cars in a couple of minutes or break into houses for quick access to money for drugs.

It wasn't long before I was in trouble again. After group sessions at the Brunswick Unit, a couple of the older guys convinced me to hang out with them. They would steal a car (their favorites back then were EH, HR, FB or FC - all Holdens) and pick me up. We would drive around and smoke dope, ending up in the paddocks of Glenroy or Broady. We would do donuts and fuck around until it got dark and then they would just torch the car in the paddock, watch it go up and then take off in another car. I loved the thrill of it.

Before too long we were caught. The two other guys were both over 16 years old with prior convictions for car thefts and other crimes and were both sentenced to two years at a youth training centre (YTC). Although I was just a passenger, the staff at the Brunswick Unit were not too impressed. Again, I became a ward of the state. Back to Turana. It was October 1974 and I was still only 14.

My family were getting fed up. My dad couldn't understand what was wrong with me and continually blamed my mother, believing that because he worked long hours while Mum was at home, she should be supervising me better. My brothers and sisters barely knew me; all they knew was that I was continually away from home, living in institutions, using drugs and alcohol, and always in some sort of trouble.

COBURG BOWLS

I couldn't go back to Collingwood Technical College after I was released from Turana for the second time. The last time I had been at the college, a couple of cops had put me in handcuffs and arrested me during assembly in front of the entire school. I had walked out with detectives on either side of me, embarrassed in a way but also feeling really important, like some hardened criminal to be feared.

So, to kill time, I began hanging around the Coburg Bowls, a pinball parlour in Sydney Road, Coburg. A huge crew congregated at the bowls, including the fighters, druggies, drinkers and criminals. Some were local and others heard its reputation and came from further away. Cops frequented the bowls daily and the cafe next door did heaps of business. I was drinking, smoking and having a laugh with whoever happened to be there (though at times I was so pilled I didn't really know what the hell was going on).

There were always plenty of girls around too. I had a reputation as a bit of a charmer and girls were happy to hang out with me and my mates. Back then the dress code was platform shoes, flares and connie cardigans. The nights were filled with excitement – girls, drugs, crimes.

Meanwhile, my family life was nearly non-existent. My Italian was hopeless and I had lost the ability to talk to my own parents. I acted like I knew what I was doing, but really I didn't have a clue.

I enrolled at Coburg Technical College but again, days spent at school were few and far between; I continually wagged to hang out at the bowls or at Coburg High School where I had become involved with a younger girl called Tracy who was very pretty. She and her close friend Kath were inseparable.

One day I asked Tracy to go out with me and her reply surprised me. She said that if she was to be my girlfriend then Kath would also have to be my girlfriend. I agreed to her unusual request and would walk around Coburg with one girl on each arm feeling pretty good about myself. I would meet them after school; sometimes together, other times separately. We would hang around the bowls or at their homes when their parents were out. Occasionally we hung out in a deserted mansion in Belgrave Street down the road from my family home. The house was empty except for the caretaker's bedroom, which came in very handy. Tracy and Kath drew the line at having a threesome so I would take it in turns to have sex with each of them.

With two girlfriends, there were moments when I felt like life couldn't get any better. But those moments were fleeting; mostly I felt like shit. I was always waiting for the next opportunity to score and the more I got, the more I wanted.

OUT OF CONTROL

By 1975, I was smoking dope constantly; it had become a daily habit. My tolerance grew. I started seeing a doctor in Nicholson Street who prescribed me Serepax, Valium, Tuinal - whatever I asked for. My dope smoking turned to pill popping: the moment I woke up I would take as many pills as I thought I needed and then I would just fall asleep wherever I went.

I wore my hair short on the top and long at the back, an early version of the mullet hairstyle. I tried to look tough by dressing like a 'sharpie', a mod look popular amongst the Carlton and Brunswick set. We wore tight tops to make ourselves look big but I was skinny and didn't fool anyone. Around that time, to my father's disgust, I also got my first tattoo, a dragon on the back of my arm.

I was hanging around at the bowls and also at a drop-in centre in Coburg. There were some good people at the drop-in centre, they would let me chill. I would come out of a sleep, look around and fall back to sleep until I had to leave because they were closing. In a daze, I would attempt to walk home and straighten up before I got there. I would have something to eat and go straight to bed. My parents were okay if I was in bed - at least they knew I was home.

I stopped going to school. There just didn't seem to be any point in keeping up the charade. I always needed money so I started selling dope and pills. Sydney Road was my stomping ground; I would walk up and down from Harding Street to Bell Street attempting to sell to people I knew. The occasional burglary also kept me in the loop on the streets.

One of my little brothers worked in a butcher shop, the other sold eggs at a store in the Coburg Market. When things got really bad, I would ask them for money. Or I'd come up with some scam to borrow or steal. Clothes shops were a favorite. I loved my clothes; sometimes, if I sold enough dope, I would even buy stuff to wear.

Because of the drugs, life was getting further out of control: the situation at home was intolerable and I started losing interest in Tracy and Kath. For a year, I drifted in a pathetic state of aimlessness.

When I was 16, I did try to pull up. My dad organised for me to work with him. He worked for a mob in the sewerage industry, digging trenches and laying pipes. The job went well, I did the work for eight long hours each day and earned good money. By day, I had my shit together. Then I'd go home, shower and eat, go out and get stoned. Sleep. Do it all again.

DENISE

Denise was a really good-looking girl I noticed outside the bowls one night. She was a bit younger than me and I really liked seeing her. I had never liked a girl as much before. One night she came past and I grabbed her in a head lock, playing around. I wanted to tell her how I felt about her but that is what I did instead.

I started going back to Denise's house to smoke dope with her brother Pat and sister Steph. Their parents never seemed to be home and it became my new hangout. When it became obvious to Denise that I had a serious habit, she tried to help by telling me she cared. She didn't know I was a hopeless case.

One morning, I was short of money and so I went to visit Denise at her place. We made out and then, when she left for school, I snuck back in and stole some money, a TV and some other stuff.

When she told me about the robbery, I totally threw her off course, made out like I knew nothing about it. Because I was stoned most of the time, I didn't experience real feelings of guilt but, deep down, I couldn't believe how low I was, breaking into the home of someone who I really liked. I stayed away for a little while.

Denise started going out with a guy named Rob. I had lost my opportunity with her but I still dropped in sometimes, usually stoned out of my head. One time, Rob answered the door and told me to fuck off. I turned around and walked away. The guy was just protecting his girlfriend. I would have done the same if I could stay straight long enough.

FIRST HIT

I was always just hanging around: Foley's, The Moreland, the Flemington flats and of course the Coburg Bowls. Occasionally I'd head to the city and hang out on the steps of Flinders Street Station. There was always somewhere to go to smoke dope, drink or just wait for something to happen. And it always did.

One afternoon I was hanging around with a guy called Browny. He was a fighter and had a reputation. We ended up in Carlton at this chick's place to score a smoke. Her name was Vicky. While we were waiting we noticed she was selling heroin, something I had managed to stay away from. We asked if we could have some and she said, "No, don't be stupid." We persisted. "Come on! Please." I wasn't 17 yet and had never injected anything but I was intrigued and thought I could just try it once. An older guy we knew walked in and told her to give us a little. We figured he knew what he was talking about and that we'd be fine.

Vicky ended up giving us a quarter of a cap for $15. The older guy hooked up a syringe, helped us mix it up and Browny and I had our first fix. It just about blew my head off. The rush was something I had never experienced before. First, euphoria took over my whole head, then I became really comfortably numb. I looked at Browny and knew he was experiencing the same thing so there was no need to ask him how he was; everything was perfect. We cleaned the fit (syringe) and anyone watching would have assumed we were experienced campaigners.

We left the house but the music stayed with me, the beat, the

FIRST HIT

smell. I lit up a smoke and it tasted great. I looked over to see Browny vomiting all over the footpath but he assured me he was okay. We caught a cab to Sydney Road, North Coburg to meet the boys. After telling the driver where we wanted to go, we didn't speak another word. The 15-minute drive was magical. I relaxed into the seat with my head tilted back. It was just getting dark and the lights overhead were flashing, the colours seemed brighter and the music in the cab enhanced the mood. The euphoric feeling was something I wanted to stay with me forever. Time seemed to disappear. Why was something that felt so good, illegal?

When we arrived at our friend Paul's unit, the boys immediately suspected something was up and asked us what was wrong. We replied at the same time, "Nothing!" We sat down and someone passed us a bong. I didn't need it but my arm automatically went out, grabbed the bong, put it to my mouth with my right hand, lit it with my left and then poked at the bowl with the match. Killed the bowl, took it all in, laid back and slowly let out the smoke. The rush again kicked in - the hit I'd had earlier. Listened to music, overheard the shit they were talking about, and let the stone take me where it did. Life felt okay: no doubts, no fear, no expectations.

Hours passed by the time I got up and said my farewells. Browny and I had experienced something together that I wanted to remember forever. I left, got a cab and went home. Snuck in the back and into my room where my elder brother was asleep. Everyone was asleep but it wouldn't have mattered, I could have faced anybody. I undressed, got into bed and lay there, feeling like I had gone to heaven.

When I woke up the nightmare I was living in was as real as

COMING CLEAN

it had ever been. However, the harsh reality of the day made the memories of the night before feel even better.

AMERICANO

My drug habit had a life of its own. Going to work was starting to get in the way; I only worked to earn the money I needed to support my using. My dad worked twice as hard as me and was paid just a little bit more - and he had to look after a family of 10. I was paid good money each Thursday and by the weekend I was broke and would be botting money from my dad to eat.

Dad and I would wake up for work each day at 5.45am and the only time I would see him sober was walking from his bedroom to the liquor cabinet to pour some whisky into his coffee. We would get ready and be picked up in an eight-seater twin-cab ute from outside the front of our house. The truck would go around picking up all the other Italian workers in the area and everyone would chat away in Italian but Dad and I wouldn't speak a word to each other. Dad knew nothing about me and I knew next to nothing about him. I knew he worked hard, that he was my dad, that he had fathered 10 children. I knew he was not very happy with his lot and that he could drink heaps. That was it. I could barely understand the Italian dialect being spoken but knew the workers were referring to me whenever they said the derogatory word, 'Americano'. They thought I spent my money like an American.

I would also have my first drink in the morning. As soon as we got to work, I would have a sip of homemade wine from Dad's flask, then drink again at morning tea and lunchtime. I was addicted to drugs, had tattoos, drank too much, had criminal convictions and was totally lost. I was pale as a ghost, gaunt with protruding cheek bones and no amount of eye drops could hide my bloodshot eyes. Dad would look at me in disgust. He had brought us from Italy to give us a better life and look how I had turned out. But as long as I turned up to work, Dad left me alone.

Meanwhile, my older brother would come home and put his pay packet on the table every week in front of everyone. My dad was proud of him. So was my mum. My dad used that money to buy a station wagon for my brother to drive the family around. I don't remember going out in it much.

Then I injured my back at work and was put on work cover. I was getting paid and no longer had to go to work, which meant I had all the time in the world to hang around, drink alcohol and use drugs.

CHARGED WITH RAPE

Maria lived down the road from me and she went to school at Mercy College in North Coburg. We started unofficially seeing each other and would meet up whenever she wagged school. One morning, I got a call from her asking if I wanted to hang out at her friend's house nearby.

When I arrived, Maria and another mate Rick were waiting outside because her friend wasn't home. Maria told me she was definitely on her way, so, thinking we could wait inside, I decided to break in. Bad move.

Once inside, I grabbed Maria and took her to the bedroom. We couldn't wait to get our clothes off. We were just getting into it when Rick started banging on the door, yelling about a group of guys out front. I jumped out of bed, had never moved so fast in all my life. Peered out the window and saw two carloads of motherfucking detectives. The house was surrounded, nowhere to run. Why did I need to run anyway? I hadn't done anything wrong, had I?

They told us to come out. Back then, every member of the armed robbery squad seemed to be handpicked for their huge size. A massive detective grabbed me, pulled me aside and asked if I had permission to be inside. Yes, of course I had permission to break in! He grabbed me around the chest area and pinned me up against the wall. They threw me and Rick into the divvy van while the other detectives talked to Maria. She appeared to be crying.

When we got to Coburg police station I was separated from

Rick and Maria. Neither of them had been involved with the police before so it was a big deal for them. But I would take the rap so no one had anything to worry about. Little did I know.

I was charged with house breaking, being on the premises unlawfully, trespassing, and, unbelievably, three counts of rape. When I had seen Maria crying she was being asked what we had been doing in the house. She told them we were waiting for her friend. Then she was asked how old she was. Fifteen. Did we have sex? Yes. How many times had we ever had sex? Three times. Because she was under age and I was nearly 17, I needed her parents' consent. No, I didn't have that. I was granted bail and our parents were called to collect us.

I considered Maria to be my girlfriend and thought that if we wanted to have sex it was no one's business. Wrong again. Her dad was fucking ropeable. Unbelievably, he was talking marriage - his poor daughter. He was in constant contact with my parents. I was shitting myself and tried to lay low for a while. I lost contact with Maria and never knew what she had to go through.

I was a convicted criminal with priors for crimes against society and serious charges pending. That's who everyone thought I was and that was how I behaved. In reality I was a scared, illiterate kid in need of help but too proud and immature to verbalise this to anyone.

Every time I was charged with an offence I would pull my head in until the heat was off, then I would carry on like nothing had happened. My injury improved and I was back to working with my dad during the day, and at night I was drinking at Foley's Pub and smoking copious amounts of dope. I got involved with guys much older than me who would give me as much as I wanted on tick. The weekends were more of the same. Friday night would come, I'd finish work about 3pm, go straight home, shower, shave, get picked up, score some gear and on to the pub. I was making a mess of my life with drugs but I couldn't live without them.

PART THREE - PRISON
1977 - 1984

COURIER

An old mate of mine from the bowls, Mario was a member of the infamous Melbourne Bank Gang. Before he was locked up for 12 years for armed robbery, he was the best-dressed bank robber in town. He carried a gun, drove a nice sports car and had plenty of women and money. I idolised Mario so I was pleased when I received a call from one of his associates. Mario had a regular job for me. I was told to go to an address in Carlton, pick up a package and take it in to Mario in Pentridge B Division.

I did everything that I was asked; however, due to my drug taking, I was unreliable. The more my drug use spiralled out of control, the more I began taxing the packages. I would take out a bit for me, re-wrap it and take it in. Originally, no one knew as I would only take out a little, but then I started taking a little more, until the whole package became mine.

Mario and some of the boys had heard that I was out of control and were not happy. These were hardened criminals I was dealing with. Knowing what it was like to be addicted to drugs didn't matter to them. They saw themselves as bank robbers and they didn't burn their mates. I came up with this cock-and-bull story that I was being watched and I was busted with a parcel. I didn't think they would believe me. But luckily, they did.

ARMED ROBBERY

Times were desperate. The only time I felt like I was coping was when I was using heroin, which I did regularly.

I was hanging around with Nicky and Andrew. We started talking about armed robberies as the burgs and stuff we were doing weren't getting us too far. Andrew and some of his mates had already committed a few armed robberies and had got away with them. At times, they would brag about how easy they were. The point was, drugs were taking over my life and I had to do something quick to make big money.

At one stage I'd briefly worked as a storeman for a children's clothes company in Lygon Street, Brunswick. I knew the running of the place. Nicky was in, Andrew was in and we got another guy called Marty to drive. I wasn't planning to be actively involved; I was too closely linked. We watched the place for a while and observed that an armoured car would drop the pay off on Thursday mornings just before 11am.

On the day of the robbery, Nicky and Andrew ran into the office with a sawn-off double barrel shotgun immediately after the armed van had dropped off the money and before it had been placed in the safe. They demanded the cash and were handed two trays of pay packets. They left the office, ran down the street, turned left, got into Marty's mini that had been parked around the corner and drove to Pascoe Vale.

I made sure I was doing something else with someone else at that time so that I had an alibi. However I could hear the sirens

ARMED ROBBERY

and sure enough, over the radio I heard that an armed robbery had occurred. A little later we all met at Andrew's house in Pascoe Vale. It had gone off well with no one getting hurt. We counted the money and gave Marty $500; he was happy and left. Nicky, Andrew and I got the rest. Andrew said he would burn the gear used to commit the robbery.

We went to the North Melbourne flats, scored some heroin, smoked some dope and kicked back in a motel, thinking we had arrived. We were it and a bit. We mulled up, had a taste and all got very stoned. We stayed at the motel for a couple of days and caught cabs to go drinking at the Quarry Hotel in Lygon Street, Brunswick. We did some stupid things at the Quarry: drank too much and shouted drinks for everyone. We were leaving to score in cabs and then returning in cabs and people started to notice our spending habits. It didn't take long before the heat caught up with us. We hadn't really split the money, just spent it.

We had been at the Quarry one morning, had a few drinks and crossed the road to the Romantica Cafe which belonged to Nicky's dad. Word got to me that the armed robbery squad had just raided my parents' house in Belgrave Street and that my dad was ropeable and looking for me. We talked about taking off but just as we were about to leave, cops swarmed over the place; we were surrounded. There were too many of them and we were too affected (well I was anyway). I was slammed to the floor and handcuffed. Nicky and Andrew were too.

As we were being walked out with our arms behind our backs, I saw my dad outside the café. He was as angry as I'd ever seen him. As I went past he said in Italian, "I don't know how you live with yourself, you bastard." I didn't respond. What could I say? I didn't know how I lived with myself either.

We were put in separate divvy vans and taken to the Brunswick police station in Sydney Road where the cops already knew me - the same detectives had charged me with rape.

Nicky had some form and knew what to do in the cop shop; Andrew - I wasn't sure. I was questioned and stuck to my story: I wasn't there, I had an alibi. But they knew I'd worked there and they'd found the gear at Andrew's place - balaclavas, gloves, the shotgun - prints all over them. He had never bothered to get rid of them. Using drugs and committing crimes doesn't mix.

By the end of the night we were all charged with armed robbery. We were refused bail and locked up in the cells. I still had a few pills and a little heroin in my pocket so I swallowed it all. We were put in separate cells but could still talk to each other. We tried to work out what had gone wrong. Absolute fucking idiots, the lot of us: using, drinking, shouting everyone cabs. All a block away from the place we had robbed.

We were fucked. Charged, with other charges pending, 18 years old and in the adult system. We were kept in the cells for a couple of days before we were transferred to Pentridge's D Division by van. The ride there was intense. I was angry as all fuck; at who I wasn't sure, we were all blaming each other. The drugs had worn off and I started hanging out on my way to jail.

PENTRIDGE

Bad night's sleep. Woke up with the realisation that I was in prison and was fucked. The fog started to lift and the paranoia set in. During my time out there using I had lied, cheated, robbed and even taxed the parcels of 'mates' I was visiting on the inside (until I didn't bother visiting at all because there was no parcel left).

Thoughts rushed through my head: what should I say? What would I do if confronted by Mario and his mates? Fear gripped me. I also started to feel a little crook from having no drugs; my body ached, pains in the guts. Didn't know whether to dry retch or sit on the toilet. Tried both. Put my name down to see the doctor. The noise of doors opening, the clunk of locks turning, the sound of prisoners calling to each other… it was getting closer and closer.

Finally pulled myself together. Prison was no place to show fear. I decided to act as if all was well. Walked down the tier in D Division, prisoners in front of me, prisoners behind me. Just followed the others. Finally went down the stairs, passing some prisoners dressed in white overalls known as 'billets' - prisoners allocated tasks like preparing meals, cleaning, basically doing something useful with their time.

We were directed into separate yards. I was put in the boys' yard next to the remand yard. Then there was the trial yard and lastly, the bone yard where pedophiles were put for their own protection - glad I wasn't in there.

The boys' yard was the shape of a huge triangle, the gate at the closed end. As I walked in there was a high blue stone wall to the right and concrete seats spaced five meters apart until the bottom wall. In the right corner there was a urinal and three open toilet bowls separated by a metre high wall and in open view to the wardens. Towards the middle there was a covered area with two heaters hanging down with seats and a few tables with steel seats bolted to the concrete floor. Further towards the left were four open showers where prisoners washed and sinks with shiny metal as mirrors.

Prisoners spent most of the day pacing up and down. The four of us, who had been locked up together, tried to stick together; we discussed our case, watched each other's backs. But on that first morning, I wasn't feeling too good - the pains were getting worse, couldn't eat breakfast. I stayed behind while the others walked in for the meal; just lay on the concrete bench barely able to move.

Time seemed to stand still until prisoners filed back in, some complaining about the shit they called breakfast, others laughing, and others just putting one foot in front of the other.

I heard my name called over the loud speaker to see the doctor so I filed down the tier following the yellow line, took my place in the queue until I was finally called in. The doctor questioned me about my condition and I did what I could to scam as much medication from him as possible. The guy probably got scammed by every prisoner trying to do their time as easily as they could. Drugs are worth heaps in prison - always were and always will be. The best l could do was secure a few painkillers three times a day and a sleeper at the end of the day - no point complaining, better than a kick in the arse.

The first dose took the edge off but that was about it. The day inched by, minute by minute. Lunch came and went, the food not worth eating. The afternoon also finally went by, had my afternoon medication, mixed with people I knew and some that I'd just met. Tea time was 3pm. Then prisoners started frantically running around to burn off energy with just half an hour before we would be locked up in our cells. I was looking forward to that time as it meant the day would be over.

The gravity of my situation hit me hard. The talk in the yard was that prisoners charged with armed robbery were getting sentences from three to seven years. Because I had an alibi, I decided to plead not guilty and take my chances.

Finally, muster was called (the checking and counting of prisoners) and then it was time for lock up. We filed in like cattle; we had to stand at the door of our cells to be checked before we were told to step inside. The noise of the door closing was initially a relief - to be on my own. Then the pain of the loneliness hit me – fuck!

I lay on my bed - a single mattress, a sheet and a couple of blankets - the medication barely making a difference. I'd had two days in the police cells plus one day in prison; I was already onto my third day with no hard drugs and who knew how much longer I would be here. Thoughts flooded my mind: my pathetic family life; my girlfriends; friends; my life falling around me - what life?; the progression from boys' homes to adult prison. If only I had something to medicate myself or relieve the pain. My mind chattered like never before. My pain wasn't physical, it was my piercing self-pity that was hurting me. My problem was drugs - the getting, using and then turning to crime to get more. And my solution was more drugs to numb the pain that they had caused in the first place.

Time started to get away from me, the day got dark. Occasionally the noise of a pigeon broke the noise in my head for the briefest moment. It was the longest day of my life. A knock at the door, the trap door opened, and my medication was handed to me by someone dressed in a white coat. Straight down it went; I willed the effect to hit but nothing happened and it was hours before I finally fell asleep. Vivid dreams: cops, running, guns, drugs.

The clunking noise of locks and doors opening woke me. Sweat all over me as reality hit all over again; this was my life on remand. I was in a cell that was six by nine feet. There was a single bed and a toilet without a seat. And that was it. To wash my hands I had to use the hose connected to the toilet bowl.

The first week was insane, crazy, no way out, detoxing in a cell. Freezing, the occasional sweats, the cramps, the feeling that my skin was two sizes too small. No one to scam or manipulate. Only one choice - lie there and go through it. Still my mind raced: how did I end up here?

The days turned into weeks; the physical detox was finally over but the mental torment continued. Prison life was something you either accepted or fought. I accepted my lot but remained furious at myself and frustrated by my powerlessness.

Attempted to apply for bail: no luck. The judge's comments rang in my ear, "A danger to yourself and society - you will stay incarcerated until further notice." Fuck you too.

USING INSIDE

The desire to use was so intense that prisoners usually found a way. Joints were around; pills were available; powders too if you had the money and knew the right people. I had no money, however I did know people. Still, I wasn't sure how many of my contacts I had burned when ripping off those parcels when I had been on the outside. The paranoia and anticipation were, at times, unbearable.

Then one afternoon I was called over the PA system, "Leonard Ottone, to the circle." My mind raced: it could be a visit from my lawyer, or cops either wanting to interview me for other crimes, or busting me for trying to get gear in.

My old friend Mario from B Division had got word that l was in remand and had come over. When l first noticed him, my heart sank. I tried to keep my composure and was relieved when a hint of a smile appeared on his hardened face; as we got close he grabbed me and gave me a brotherly hug. He asked if l was okay under the circumstances and I was so relieved that he wasn't pissed at me, I told him I was A-okay.

Mario knew the scene better than anyone. He told me I had upset a few people that didn't need upsetting; I'd ripped off the wrong people. I didn't bother denying anything; the best I could do was say I was fucked and desperate and couldn't really remember what l had done or to who. Junkies had a bad reputation but he seemed to appreciate my honesty.

Once that was out of the way, the conversation turned to the robbery that had landed me in prison; he told me that the talk was that we had done more robberies and still had access to money. Not the case. I was as broke as I'd ever been and in more trouble than the early settlers. He asked if l needed anything and of course I took the opportunity to ask if he had anything on him. He burst out laughing and told me l had more front than Myers. The screw walked over to tell us the visit was over. No worries, boss. As we got up to walk away, Mario hugged me again and slipped me a small parcel; immediately I felt the stress of jail disappear.

The parcel was a block of hash. Couldn't wait to get locked up in my cell for the night; didn't say anything to anyone, just made sure I had the essentials - tobacco, papers, and water. The time finally came for lock up: lined up, checked, counted, door locked. It was smoking time and I knew I had to be really careful with the screws walking up and down the tier.

The hash smelt absolutely sensational as I broke off a piece and spread it on the bed of tobacco, rolled a paper, sealed it, put the filter in. Stood as close to the window as I could and lit her up. The rush of good hash went straight to my head, took a deep breath, held on, closed my eyes, and… wow. The prison bars melted, the blue stone and cold left me, replaced with a warm feeling of contentment; I needed more and two joints turned into three. Then I had to put it out as the stone overtook me. Blew the smoke towards the window then lay on the bed letting my mind do its thing; stoned as a maggot was the way to do your time. It wasn't too long before I lit her up again and off I went into a dream-like state. The night disappeared.

Morning: the noise of doors unlocking, prisoners talking - some happy to see their mates, some unhappy to be waking up in prison

USING INSIDE

one more day. My turn: door unlocked, I'd already had a few drags and couldn't help smiling when I saw my mates. They immediately knew I had been smoking and wanted in.

KILLING TIME

Getting tattooed by a cellmate was one way to kill time. I would sit there night after night while someone pricked my skin with a needle wrapped in cotton wool and dipped into ink - dot, dot, dot... The amateur images, skulls and crossbones, were crap but I didn't care; I didn't make good decisions on the outside, I wasn't about to start now. We knew nothing about AIDS and we didn't give a second's thought to the risk of contracting hepatitis from using the filthy needles that we sharpened on the concrete and shared. Big mistake. Later, I would cover the pathetic tattoos with huge elaborate professional tattoos that also masked the track marks in my arms and other scars.

There were no televisions in our cells so some of the prisoners would read books to deal with the mind-numbing boredom of life on remand. I could barely read the letters I occasionally received from family and friends on the outside.

Somehow my learning issues had slipped under the radar. The problem was of my own making; a result of my inability to let people know I was struggling, choosing to wag school instead. While in the juvenile justice system I was asked if I wanted to attend school, and I had said no - my pride got in the way. I didn't want to be labelled as dumb, it was bad enough I already wore the labels 'drug addict' and 'criminal'.

My illiteracy was really starting to affect me and finally I sought help from some of the other prisoners who taught me how to decipher the letters. I began to read whatever I could; at times I found simple books and other times I just attempted to de-code single words. I also began to write short letters. Again, I found other prisoners willing to help me. I learnt more about reading and writing from other prisoners than any teacher.

Writing letters became a priority and I wrote as much as I could. Some prisoners who didn't have anyone to write to would give me their allocation of letters. There really wasn't much to write about, I certainly didn't write about how I felt as I had no clue. I used a lot of swear words, not to be rude but to join other words together so that I could make a sentence. I don't know how much of my letters were understood; my words formed a continuous stream of consciousness with no punctuation whatsoever.

SERVING A SENTENCE

Life on remand was monotonous; the days turned into weeks and then months. Doing time: bars, walls, barbed wire, prisoners, wardens, sirens, bells, locks, drugs, bashings, the occasional rape of an inmate by a violent prisoner, visits, letters, hopes of release, disappointment.

We were given dates for our court cases: November 1978 in the County Court of Victoria. I had to settle for a Legal Aid lawyer because there was no money to hire a private lawyer and I was the only one pleading not guilty. Nicky and Andrew were sentenced to seven years with a minimum of five, while the driver got four years with a two-year minimum.

My trial lasted for seven days. I was found not guilty for the actual armed robbery but guilty on accessory before and after the fact and was given four years with a minimum of two. With time already served, that meant about one more year in prison, depending on the parole board. Fucking spewing.

Soon afterwards, there was a committal hearing on the Maria rape charges. The charges were reduced and I pleaded guilty to carnal knowledge. I was sentenced to one month imprisonment to be served concurrently with the armed robbery sentence.

With all the cases out of the way, I started to focus on getting out. I was transferred to A Division for a few months, then to Bendigo Prison where I was to remain for the rest of my sentence. Serving a sentence was better than killing time on remand. It was also less boring, with more activities on offer and a gym where I could work out.

SERVING A SENTENCE

It was a different prison, but the yard politics were all the same. The most important rule was universal: don't react even when someone is being bashed to death in front of you. Luckily I had a few mates there, we stuck together, looked out for each other.

The routine in Bendigo was the usual: wake up, tidy the room, wash up, muster, then off to various jobs. I mostly got out of doing any work and I was left to my own devices. I spent most of my time working out in the gym, smoking dope and enjoying the occasional hit of heroin or whatever else I could lay my hands on. The visits kept me going, one of my brothers would bring me some dope and that would get me through most of the week. I also made friends based on who would be a good source of drugs, like Dave whose wife buried dope in the garden where he worked.

Finally the date of my release rolled around. A mate called Andrew who I'd met in the prison system met me at the gate. In spite of how I'd ended up in prison in the first place, and all the introspection and lessons I thought I'd learned, within minutes of my release I found myself mixing a hit of heroin. Family and loved ones were forgotten. All the promises I'd made to myself were mixed in, sucked up into the syringe and injected into my arm. The warm feeling engulfed me and overpowered any decent intentions; before I knew it, I had already breached a parole condition. I'd served 18 months of a four-year sentence, leaving me with two and a half years' parole. I was supposed to report within a day of being released. That didn't happen. Four days passed before I realised I was still in Bendigo using heroin, having unprotected sex with a girl I didn't know, not eating and making no contact with my family or friends. That was me, thinking I was in control.

KAREN & CHANTELLE

When I finally made it back to Melbourne I went to report to my parole officer and made up some cock-and-bull story about where I'd been. I was given a warning that I would be breaching parole if I didn't take things seriously. No worries.

I began popping pills: Valium, Serepax, Mandies and whatever I could get my hands on. Drank copious amounts of alcohol and dabbled in powders.

One night I ended up at a flat in East Brunswick where a couple, Karen and Matt, lived. Matt went out and I started talking to Karen. Before I knew it I was flirting with her and had convinced her that I liked her. She told me that Matt was abusive and that she wanted to break up with him but she was scared of how he would react. Over the next couple of weeks our relationship developed and being with me gave her the confidence she needed to end the relationship with Matt.

Matt moved out and we couldn't pay the rent so Karen and I moved into my parents' house in Coburg. Staying there again put a strain on everyone: I had just been released from prison; I was stoned out of my mind most of the time; and I was living with a girl I hardly knew.

My parents were not very happy about any of it. Life was not supposed to be like this. In prison, I'd decided to make something of myself and to make my family proud of me. Instead I was an embarrassment to everyone.

Karen and I eventually moved into a commission flat in West

KAREN & CHANTELLE

Brunswick and before too long she became pregnant. We decided to keep the baby but the pregnancy stressed us both out (for obvious reasons) and we started arguing.

I went back to digging trenches with my dad but, before long, I hurt myself again and found myself back on work cover; my back was killing me and the painkillers the doctor prescribed were a form of opioid. Yet another drug took over my life. The only solace in my life seemed to be mood and mind-altering substances.

Karen tried to get me to change my ways. I was on the dole, getting work cover and selling dope to get me by. If there was a way to make money, I'd find it. My drug habit was costing us a lot because my tolerance was so huge.

How I survived I don't know, why she stayed was beyond me too. Being stoned was the only way I knew how to cope and I only felt the shame when I woke in the mornings - until of course I did it all again. Against all reason, Karen was hanging on to the hope that I would do something worthwhile but that just wasn't going to happen.

Then one day, Karen's waters broke and I took her to hospital in Carlton. While she was in labour, I was in and out, using in the toilets. Out of control.

Chantelle Shirley Leigh was born 12 June 1981. (Had to check that - I was so stoned at the time I could never recall her birth date.) At the age of 21, I had a little baby girl whose eyes made me melt.

Karen looked after Chantelle as best she could. But she didn't know what to do with me. I was in a bad way; my weight was at its lowest, my red eyes hung out of my head. As long as I was stoned, nothing seemed to matter, and when I wasn't stoned, I was overwhelmed by reality. I couldn't look after myself but was faking a relationship and bringing a child into a nightmare of a life. How selfish could I be?

There was no stopping me. The medication I was taking for my back was lost in the pool of other drugs I was taking daily, and I struggled to keep my appointments with parole officers, doctors, workcover officers. Cheque day and the workcover payments all went on scoring and using. I had no friends, family members looked at me with contempt, and the cops were watching me. I didn't know what to do or where to go.

Barely breathing some days. Drugs were my only comfort, when my beautiful daughter alone should have been enough. To keep out of everyone's way I ended up committing more crimes: burgs, selling drugs. Every time I thought it couldn't possibly get any worse, sure enough it did.

Every morning I woke up riddled with fear in anticipation of the day ahead. The shame and guilt was so painful I spent most of my energy trying to stay so stoned I didn't have to feel anything.

Only the safety of a cell could save my life.

BREACH OF PAROLE

My drug habit, the petty crimes and failing to report to probation officers was costing me my sanity, my freedom, my family and any shred of respect I still enjoyed amongst my peers. The drugs were not giving me the relief I needed, but still I had no way of slowing down. It all caught up with me again in the Coburg Magistrates Court.

Going to court was easy after having a hit in the morning. I walked into a small room filled with police, solicitors, barristers, prisoners, offenders. The justice system at its best. If you could afford representation you had a better chance, and if you couldn't, a Legal Aid lawyer would have to do.

Charges of dishonesty, breach of parole, drug habit, history of offending. Straight to prison. I was sentenced to six months, during which I would also be serving out my parole.

While I was stoned I wasn't too concerned; however after the sentence was passed and I was taken away and placed in the cells, my mind started the flogging - critical, judgmental, harsh. You fucking loser Leonard, how the fuck did you end up back here? The shame, the guilt. The drugs started to wear off and the reality of the situation gripped me. The process: strip searched, showered, clothed, fed and taken to D Division until I could be classified to another jail.

The screws asked if I needed a doctor and as much as I wanted to say no, I knew that was an illusion. Of course they could also see I wasn't doing too well. The wait to see the doctor seemed endless.

He gave me some pills and ordered that I be kept in an observation cell so they could keep tabs on me. The next few days were a blur; all I remember is trying to eat, taking medication and just lying there - sleeping, waking, falling back to sleep.

Hit a wall, totally exhausted. No energy for anything; felt like shit, looked like shit. My life was no life worth living and still the only thing I craved was drugs - not my daughter or partner or family. The drugs that had led me to hell were still my only solution to getting out of hell.

I found myself back in the exact same cell in D Division where I'd been three years previously. As I lay on the bed I looked up and there on the wall I saw the words, "Leonard was here in 1979." Felt sick to the stomach; there it was written in stone, proof that I was repeating my mistakes, living my nightmare over and over. I climbed up and scratched the words off the wall - never in my wildest dreams did I think I'd be back in the same cell, desperately erasing something I'd once proudly written.

Time is not a friend of mine. Never has been. I was always waiting: waiting to get out, waiting for relief, never satisfied. The feelings of withdrawal took over. After about a week I starting to come good, the medication regime ended and there were no drugs left in my system.

A couple of months later, I was classified to Ararat prison, a three-hour drive from Melbourne. Just before I was transferred, my workers' compensation claim case arising from the injury sustained to my back when I worked with Dad, was settled. I was given just $15,000 after evidence was presented from my burglary trial that I had been able to carry TV sets out of houses. In other words, my back wasn't too badly damaged after all.

In Ararat I moved into a cell with two blokes. Didn't stay long in that particular cell as a vacancy came up with my friend Mario and another bloke called Vince; they were the head cooks in the prison and enjoyed special privileges, including access to food whenever they wanted.

Despite the long drive from Melbourne, Karen visited each Saturday with Chantelle. Visiting days were also an opportunity to score from Enzo, a dedicated supplier who would come each week to 'visit' his cousin in prison. Visitors were rarely strip-searched so he would sneak in a gram or two of heroin inside his clothing. I would go out to greet Karen and Chantelle, stay a few minutes and keep an eye out for Enzo. As soon as he arrived, I would greet him with a handshake and get the gear.

The hard part was always how to get the heroin from the mess hall back into the cell. Prison greens (jumpsuits) hadn't been introduced yet, so I would hide it as best I could inside my jeans. Prisoners with no visitors were put on barbecue duty and wouldn't get searched when it was time to go back in the cells. They could be a handy mule if you could pass them any drugs that had been brought to you during a visit. I made sure that I was tight with whoever was on duty on any given week.

On a couple of occasions, to Karen's disgust, I deliberately poured coffee all over my clothes so I had an excuse to go back inside to change at a moment when the screws were too busy to search me. Once inside, I'd get a syringe and mix up a taste, then hide the gear and syringe and go back out to finish the visit. Once or twice I had too much and the screws became suspicious; I was searched but they never found anything on me and couldn't work out how I'd managed to get stoned during a visit. I'd be very proud of myself, getting one over them.

I would try to make the gear last the whole week. I hid the drugs all over the prison - in small gaps formed by scraping away the mortar between the bricks in the laundry, in holes dug in the garden - anywhere I had access.

Syringes were like gold. They were harder to smuggle into the prison during visits because you had to walk through metal detectors, so the best way to get them was to build a good connection with the 'trusted prisoner' who worked in the medical centre.

After a visit, the early days of the week were a breeze. However by Wednesday or Thursday the gear had usually run out and I would start to hang out till the next visit. Enzo was a gun; he turned up every week with something to smoke or some heroin. And Karen's reliability as a visitor provided the cover I needed to put the screws off the scent.

At times I tried to keep the drugs to myself; would have a taste and chill. Other times, I would sell a few caps, make a couple of hundred and use it to score the following week. As a result, I was a pretty popular guy in prison. However, some crooks were totally against users. We were considered untrustworthy and I was told by certain influential inmates not to bother going to particular cells to visit as I would be red-lighting them. These were people you didn't fuck around with.

Because of the money I made selling drugs to other prisoners, I could afford plenty of dope to smoke as well as heroin, speed - actually whatever I wanted. Doing time was easy, not much to do. My job in the kitchen was a bogey; I either didn't turn up or turned up and did nothing. I was stoned most of the time and when I wasn't, I worked out in the gym.

Eventually, I was told that I was being transferred to the open camp, Won Wron in Gippsland; things had been heating up in the Ararat prison, drugs were rife and the screws were starting to come down hard. I felt that I was being moved just in time.

My time in Ararat had not been too bad, despite witnessing the occasional bashing and rape. Prison was - and always will be - a place where you don't say, see or hear anything; I'd lived most of my life like that. But you still occasionally heard about a tough guy breaking the golden rule and informing on a mate in exchange for a lenient sentence or to get bail.

The day I was transferred to Won Wron my excitement and relief was tinged with sadness to be leaving Mario and Vince. Just before I got into the van, I said my goodbyes, scored some bud to smoke and left. The van ride was pleasant - being stoned was the way to go. Before I knew it we had arrived; when they opened the van I was happy to see a few of my mates there waiting for me.

Hey boys, what's happening?

WON WRON OPEN CAMP

Prison is prison. It doesn't really matter where you are locked up when your freedom has been taken away. However, the minimal security facility in Won Wron, Gippsland, was a decent institution for prisoners preparing for their release back into the community.

Karen was still coming to see me but things between us were strained. I would try to convince Karen how much I appreciated all she did for Chantelle, and I would hold my little angel in my arms and squeeze her. But my eyes would be darting about, looking for another visitor and the opportunity to score. My mind would be racing – hoping, wishing for time to pass so I could get back to the safety of my cell to use whatever I'd managed to conceal in my pants.

Karen got fed up with my bullshit. One Saturday afternoon she arrived with Chantelle looking confident and happy. She had planned it well, was all dressed up. She told me she'd had enough of me and wouldn't be visiting again. The thought of not seeing my girls again for the remainder of my sentence cut deep. At the same time, I was wondering how I would score without such a reliable visitor and the resultant access to the visiting area. However, I'd had some dope so I was able to hold it together and act like I was handling things.

As the visit was coming to an end I tried to convince her to give me an opportunity to prove my loyalty. But she was spot on - I was interested in no one but myself and that wasn't going to change in a hurry. Tears welled up in my eyes and it took all my energy to hold myself back from grabbing Chantelle; I told her that I loved her and that I was sorry and her beautiful face comforted me. Then Karen said goodbye. It was so hard, knowing that she was right, that our relationship was only about my own convenience. I put my head down and hugged her and said goodbye, watched her walk away. I was caught between two competing desires – wanting her to turn around and come back and say she loved me, at the same time wanting her to hurry up and leave so I could go to my cell and have the mother of all hits.

Karen strapped Chantelle into the car, waved and drove away. On the walk back to the cell I bumped into a mate who asked, "You cool brother?" "No," I said, "dear John visit." Of course it was nothing that a gram of heroin and a couple of grams of choof couldn't fix, however I didn't tell him that as he would have followed me into my cell.

In my cell, I sat down, put my head into my hands and started to cry. Didn't know what to do – couldn't really use the heroin as I would be too stoned for muster and dinner. So I rolled a joint, sat in the brasco (toilet) and smoked the whole fucking thing – ripped off my fucking head. Made it to the sink, grabbed some eye drops to sort out my eyes, and walked outside.

The grapevine was very healthy in the prison system – only 15 minutes had passed since I'd told my mate I'd had a dear John visit and walking out of my cell I was inundated with wishes of good will and support. Yes, that's right, prisoners – humans with human feelings – wishing some fucking criminal drug addict sympathy for the loss of a relationship, with a small child involved. As stoned as I was, I appreciated the words of encouragement, even from people I believed were fucking maggots – either for the crimes they had committed or because I just assumed they were fucked. Anyhow, had to put all that aside and accept the words of support that were meant well.

In the mess room I wasn't very hungry for food; I did what I had to do then went straight back to my cell, only allowing a couple of mates in. While we waited for evening muster a few people came to the door but I told them to fuck off. I needed to be by myself; no hard feelings. Muster was called, took forever for the screws to get to my door. Just before they locked my door, the governor - the main man - put his head in and asked if I was okay. Had to be careful how I replied as the wrong answer could result in a ramp of the cell (a raid or lock-down that also involves shutting off the toilet system). I responded by joking, "Yeah gov, just a broken heart and a broken head - nothing too serious." He replied, saying someone would check on me throughout the night. "No need for that gov, not much I can do about it." I appreciated his concern but couldn't help wonder who the dog was who'd informed to the governor.

They locked the door behind us and moved on; we waited a couple of minutes to hear the faint noise of the doors locking... further and further away until the muster was complete. The sound of televisions and stereos indicated that it was time and the coast was clear. Both my cellmates Vince and Anthony were concerned about me, but I assured them I was okay.

Threw Vince a bud and told him to mull up; asked Anthony to put a bong together using a small bottle, a piece of hose, some silver foil and a rubber band. While all this was happening I went to the brasco, closed the door and proceeded to unwrap the syringe. Got the spoon out, laid all on the toilet cover, sucked some water into the syringe and immediately felt the familiar ease and comfort.

Vince yelled out, "You okay?"

"Yeah bro, just a little constipated."

In prison some people were opposed to powders and needles; Vince was one of them. I quickly unwrapped the heroin, took out a small rock, put it in the spoon, poured the water onto the rock and watched it dissolve into a clear solution. I put a filter in, sucked it up, held it up and flicked the syringe with my right finger to get the air out. Had a vein ready and in it went.

The prison, the visit, Karen, Chantelle, the gov: it all disappeared into my vein. Heroin - the mother of all painkillers. The rush went straight to my head; enough to feel, not enough to be on the nod. Wrapped everything up, got rid of all the evidence and walked back into the cell.

"You okay, bro?"

"Yeah, just not feeling too well."

Anthony passed me the bong, "Will this fix you?"

Put my right thumb over the hole at the back of the bottle, lit the bowl with my left hand and demolished the bowl; took it all in, put my head back against the chair and let the smoke out slowly, the rush kicking on the heroin I'd just had. Passed the bong back, watched it go around. The other two were not big smokers so it didn't take much to get them stoned. Cleaned up with Rodriguez in the background singing *Sugar Man*. Went back into the brasco, had another taste. Lay on the bed, thoughts racing around my head: Karen, was she gone forever? Chantelle, I would definitely see her again. Rodriguez, sugar man, won't you bring back all those colours… Faded out, slept.

REALITY HITS

Waking up was a breeze when I had gear on me. Nothing was a problem. Straight into the toilet, did the ritual, the morning taste is the couta. Being careful about how much I used was never easy for me.

Sometimes it occurred to me my addiction was about the rush rather than the substance. I honestly didn't care what drug I was using as long as I could get stoned. When I was sober, I was nothing.

Hid all the evidence, got the choof out, made a mix and woke up the others.

"What's up bro?"

"Not much, couldn't sleep. Ya want a brew?"

"Yeah, thanks mate."

"Anthony, you want a drink?"

"Yeah, thanks mate."

"Sorry for waking you guys, have a pipe."

That was life in open camp when you had gear.

The sound of doors unlocking, one by one, the screws were getting closer. Had to get rid of all the evidence; the effect of the heroin was a bit much, then smoking as well. The guys let me know that I wasn't looking too good. I decided to take a sicky; the screws would be cool. As soon as our door opened I went down to the circle where the screws congregated.

"Hey boss, not feeling the best. Gonna stay in today."

"No worries, make sure you get a cover for the laundry."

"No worries."

REALITY HITS

Dumb fucks wouldn't know what to look for, my eyes were practically rolling in the back of my head. The next few days were the same: stoned, thinking about Karen and Chantelle. Wasn't too bad while I was stoned, but I knew that as soon as the gear ran out I was going to be in a lot of bother. Had a few great days in my cell, on my own, stoned, having a taste every few hours; friends checked in from time to time to make sure I had all that I needed. One close friend, Liam came to see me and could tell I had been using.

"You look off your head, brother. Good gear, hey?"

"Yeah, it's alright; you want a taste?"

"Mate, does Dolly Parton sleep on her back? You fucking beauty Lenny, you're a gun."

"Only got a bit bro, so between me and you."

"Yeah mate, yeah sweet."

The ritual began: the syringe, the water, filter, and of course the main ingredient, the big H – heroin. Seeing Liam so fixated on the hit that we were preparing made me realise how consumed I could be: eyes lit up, body erect, fully focused on the rush to come. It briefly occurred to me that if I put that much attention into my life, I might achieve something worthwhile!

Liam had a taste and immediately felt the effect.

"Thanks mate, you're a gun Lenny."

"No worries Liam, any time."

That wasn't really true; I would only share as long as it didn't affect my taste.

We sat and talked for a while. He was doing the last bit of lagging (his sentence) for a violent assault. Didn't know what he was going to do when he got out, he hadn't heard from his girl for a while, worried he was going to lose it when he got back out there.

"Just gotta keep your cool, don't do nothing stupid. You gotta put yourself in her shoes bro, five years is a long time."

I was not really in any position to be offering advice, besides this was just heroin talk. We would probably forget this conversation by the time the stone wore off.

Soon enough Liam left for muster. I had another taste and hid the rest of the gear outside the cell just in case the screws decided to ramp it, all the while keeping an eye out for the dogs (informers). There was the danger of getting too stoned, could risk overdosing, or just nodding off and being busted. Could even set off a ramp of the whole prison, didn't want that, could upset people who liked doing time in an open camp.

The week went by and the gear finally ran out; had some dope to smoke for a few days but that wasn't cutting it, so in desperation I tried ringing Karen to see if she would visit. No luck. Fuck!

It was time to face what I had been putting off. I knew the dope would eventually run out and I was going to have to deal with reality. I was either stoned and okay, or straight and not so okay; that was about all I knew. And right then I was one angry, sick motherfucker and I couldn't do a thing about it. The amount of heroin I had used in the last week had given me a habit and I was crook: spewing, dry retching, cramps, the runs, flu-like symptoms which felt like they were going to kill me. They hadn't before, but this time I was convinced I would die. Pathetic.

The guys came back to the cell and were not sure what was going on: as far as they could tell I was smoking dope one minute, and sick as a dog the next.

"What's going on man, you look like shit. You okay?"

"Not really man, fucking crook. Think I'm coming down with something."

"You want me to mull up a smoke?"

"Nuh, not really man."

"You sure you're okay - not like you to knock back a smoke."

"I know man, I'm crook."

"Can we do anything for ya?"

"Nuh man, I'll be right. I'll see if anyone's got anything to help out."

"We know you've been using Leonard, don't fucking bang on about being crook. You want to use drugs, that's your business. Just don't fucking talk shit to us."

"Sorry mate, I know how you feel about the powders."

"Yeah, but fuck man you've been off your face all fucking week. What do we do if you overdose or something?"

"I won't OD."

"How do you fucking know until you put the shit in your arm?"

"Okay, okay. I'm sorry man."

Anthony went for a walk and came back with a slab of sleepers (sleeping tablets).

"Thanks brother, they got any more?"

"Mate, don't push it. It's just about time for muster - get some more in the morning."

The pills worked well combined with a few bongs and I was out like a light. In the morning I threw down a few more pills, had a pipe; could barely get up. The guys both said to stay in bed; they went to the screws and gave a spiel that I had been up all night dry retching.

People kept checking in, the days went by. The heroin was all gone and the dope had dried up completely. Got through the horrors with the help of a few pills. Tried to phone Karen a few times with no luck. Eventually I got hold of my younger brother Sam. He had always been there for me, bailing me out, lending me money; he agreed to come for a visit the following weekend. My feelings were still very raw. The reality was I wasn't getting what I wanted. What was it that I wanted, exactly? Everything - my way. No chance, Leonard.

RED ALERT

Saturday morning: woke, cleaned up, went for a walk, came back to the cell, woke the guys up with a brew and was ready for the day. The weekends in prison, and in particular the open camp, were spent getting ready for visits or befriending people who had visits. Few of the prisoners went in for lunch as the families brought much better food.

My brother Sam rocked up with his girlfriend Robyn and we sat and talked for a while, got the news about Mum, Dad, and everyone else. I had become estranged from my family since my time living in boys' homes, on the streets, and in prison. Still, according to Sam, I was always remembered in my family's prayers, mainly my mum's, bless her soul. Sam had a good head on his shoulders; he ran his own business, had a girl he loved and was one of my favorite brothers. Totally appreciated him visiting and while in the visiting area managed to score half an ounce of budda from another 'visitor' that would get me through a few weeks. Told my brother to tell Karen I missed her and that if she was fucking around, to remind her I was getting out soon.

Visiting time ended. Back to the cell to wait for muster and the day to end. Got out the dope, thinking about taking a little out and hiding the rest outside the cell before lockup. Must have been on autopilot as I just started mulling up without pulling the curtains – in full view of outside. Walker, a dog of a screw, walked past, saw me mulling the mix and started barking like a dog. He immediately locked the cell door. I had nowhere to go, I was on my own. So I calmly had a few bongs and waited for the cavalry.

My cell was put on red alert – anyone who approached would be grabbed so everyone stayed away. Decided to flush the dope, as I was supposed to be getting out soon and didn't want to ruin my chances of being released. A moment after I flushed it, they turned the water off. Then I proceeded to pull the bong apart. The screws were at my cell door in numbers, batons out ready for the ramp. As they opened the door, the effect of the dope hit me like a ton of bricks.

Four screws forced their way in; a little extreme, I thought. Told me to put my hands behind my back. I started to laugh; I was in prison being asked to put my hands behind my back. The screws didn't find it too humorous.

They locked my cell and proceeded to pull it to bits. Had nothing to worry about, the dope was gone; the only thing they found was an empty bottle with a hole in it. I was escorted to the isolation cell, the door closed behind me, ringing in my ears. There was no bed so I lay down on the mat on the floor.

My mate Vince brought me my dinner. "Mate, what the fuck happened?"

Thought they might be listening so I said, "Fucked if I know."

When I knew there was no one around, I asked Vince to go check the sewerage pit to see if it caught the dope.

Figured I had a chance of getting off as they'd only found a bottle with a hole in it, which is not actually a crime. Thought I'd be left in the lockup cell overnight and would have to wait till Monday morning for the gov. Fucking Walker the dog, thought he'd busted the crime of the century. I was now in a cell within a cell, under lockdown. No dope, no wife, no friends, in the middle of fucking Gippsland, no idea what tomorrow would bring.

Time dragged; a couple of people stuck their necks out and yelled out hello when walking past. Sunday night muster: Liam brought me my meal while the screw stood right behind him. Told me to check the food before eating anything. A smile immediately appeared on my face; I knew what that meant. Sure enough, a massive joint had been hidden under the chips. Put the food down; could only eat that shit when stoned. I lit her up and blew the smoke out the window - only needed a few tokes, would try to make it last all night.

Monday morning I was anxious to face the gov and sort this shit out. Around 10am I heard the noise of keys clinking and voices approaching. Yep, this was it. Door opened; the look on Walker's face was priceless - he was salivating. No wonder the screws are called dogs! Handcuffed and escorted to the gov's court, basically a kangaroo court that would decide my fate. Walked in, the gov sitting behind a desk, screw on either side, another near the door, and one more outside. Again a little extreme - they told me that was policy. The charges were read out: possession of drugs and drug paraphernalia. I got 60 days loss of privileges to be served in H Division, Pentridge. Immediate transfer. I was totally dumbfounded.

"You fucking piece of shit."

The governor responded by telling his pathetic soldiers to take me away, hands cuffed behind my back. I was grabbed by my hands and they were lifted a little so I had to walk on my toes. No use making it any harder on myself.

Fucking H Division, could it get any worse? Taken back to the observation cell until the van was ready to take me away. Fuck!

THE RIDE TO H DIVISION

I was escorted to the van. A few friends were there to say goodbye from a distance. The heavy door slammed behind me and the lock and key did their thing. It took a few seconds to adjust to the darkness of the van.

The ride in the cold dark van from Won Wron to Coburg's Pentridge Prison took about three hours and felt like forever. It was horrific: one, I was going to the infamous H Division; two, dumped by Karen; three, no fucking drugs. I had no idea what was about to happen. Fucking kicked myself. You dickhead. Plastic gangsta. Hey, dipstick.

The familiar noise of the microphone, "Van up, van up". The sound of the roller door opening and the voices of the screws doing their routine bullshit to justify their existence. The van moved again, stopped, moved again. Then, moved through the prison until it came to a halt. Unfamiliar noises of wardens talking in code. The handover was short; cuffs removed and I was told to walk inside.

I was paralysed by fear. Sweating like never before. I was told to get undressed. Six huge motherfucking screws stood a foot apart from each other until there was a circle around me. Nowhere to go. I could hear I was being yelled at but had no idea what was being said. Something along the lines of, "Welcome to H Division, these are the rules, step out of line and suffer the full force of the law". Found myself nodding to their assertive tone. Fucking cocksuckers, I thought. But it was only ever going to be a thought; just a few months to go and the possibility of parole, even that was now at risk. Nodded my head and proceeded in the direction I was pointed.

Never felt so safe walking into a cell in all of my life. The door finally closed behind me; nothing in the cell but a bed and the brick walls, a thick door, a small barred window and me, alone.

Having gone from shooting heroin in an open camp to the infamous H Division - the H obviously standing for hell, a place where the toughest of men had been broken and used as examples of powerlessness - I had moved from almost freedom to solitary confinement.

This was a wake-up call. But I couldn't help thinking that a taste would not go astray. Right now, now, now, now, now, now.

60 DAYS

H Division was best known as the home of Chopper Read and other inmates who chopped off their body parts. I had never expected to end up in Pentridge's most notorious unit because I didn't consider myself to have anything in common with blokes like that. H Division was rock bottom.

Solitary confinement was not for the weak-hearted. Once I got over the initial shock of having been sent there, the fear totally immobilised me. I was 25 years old but with the maturity of a 15-year-old; I felt like a young boy in a man's prison. The cells were dark and cold and the ceiling was covered in mesh, just like a cage. It had the desired impact, I felt like an animal.

My crime: possession of drug paraphernalia - an empty bottle of orange juice suspected of being used as a bong.

H Division the first morning: I was awakened by the sound of clunking keys rattling, locks, doors opening; the noise getting closer and closer to my cell. The night's sleep had not been very pleasant - tossed and turned most of the night, the occasional sound of people yelling obscenities and barking at one another: "You fucking dog [Chopper] Read, maggot dog." People banging loudly for no other reason but to make noise, get some attention.

The cell door finally opened. The wardens were massive men, handpicked for this place they called the justice system. Strip-searched by two aggressive motherfuckers barking instructions to follow certain yellow lines marked on the floor which seemed to be heading to nowhere. The wardens yelled at me to step it up, then slow it down, playing fucking mind games. I was marched to a yard that appeared to be smaller than any other yard I had ever seen. It was about six by six metres; three of the walls were bluestone and the other wall was made of wire mesh.

Only me in the yard. The door closed behind me with a clunk, the two wardens talked to each other as they walked away, their voices fading into the bluestone walls, the faint noise of a radio in the background - *Smooth Operator* - didn't feel so smooth in prison. Started pacing up and down with nowhere to go, my mind racing. What to do? How to act? What to say? Was I going to see anyone? Just then, cell doors opened and closed, I could hear voices. Couldn't make out what was being said. It must be breakfast. A billet (a prisoner dressed in white) opened the yard door and handed out the food while flanked by two other huge screws. Cold toast, lukewarm porridge and a cup of coffee. The door closed behind me with a thud. Drinking the cup of coffee, I started to think a cigarette would be nice. Just as the thought passed, a shoelace with something attached appeared to be crawling down the wall. I began to get paranoid, thinking I was being set up, didn't know what to do. It came to a halt and then a voice said, "Are you going to take it or not?" Before I could think, I reached out and grabbed the parcel. Still had no idea what, who or why this had just happened. I quickly opened the small parcel. The shoestring disappeared back over the wall. Awesome. The parcel contained four small rolled cigarettes, a match that was split in four and a small scratch to light the smoke. Put one to my lips, took a match and lit the smoke. Deep breath. Unbelievable. Never knew a cigarette could taste so good. After I digested the food and smoked the cigarette there was nothing to do but pace: six steps one way, then six steps the other. Who the fuck was that? Anyway, truly appreciated the thought. Someone obviously knew about solitary confinement. Thanks heaps whoever that was.

I paced for most of the day, stopping occasionally to do sit ups, pushups, then more pacing. My mind continually raced. Would I hear from Karen? Would I see Chantelle? The loss of privileges really hit home. This was as bad as it got: the strip searches, being paraded, nowhere to go, no one to talk to. Who cared about me? No one. The stranger who threw the shoelace over the wall cared, I thought briefly. I had to smoke all the cigarettes because I knew I was going to be searched again. What to do about my life? The time on my own gave me plenty of opportunity to think.

The days in H Division turned to weeks. Karen finally contacted me and wanted to visit. The visit was unlike any I'd had before - a box visit, me on one side of the glass, Karen and Chantelle on the other, a warden by my side. The visit was supervised and I was informed it could be cancelled any time I said anything inappropriate. So the conversation was kept to: How are you going? Why did you visit? Karen said, "Why do you think? You're the father of my child. And I wanted to know if you were okay." Yeah, I'm okay. Needed to pull my head in anyway. I attempted to say sorry. Karen said not to bother.

Chantelle kept calling out my name, "Daddy, Daddy." Sad for a father to hear that through glass; couldn't touch her. Miss you so much baby. I love you.

The visit ended and again, I had to watch Karen turn around with Chantelle and walk away. I was escorted to my cell. Again, the screws were behind me. Some stayed right up your arse; others kept their cool.

The days were short. Spent from 7am till 3pm in the closed yard and the remaining time in a locked cell. No books, no cigarettes, no contact, only the occasional letter or visit.

The time in H Division finally came to an end. Parole had been granted. I would be transferred to A Division to serve another two months before being released to the community with another six months to serve on parole – the system's way to keep tabs on me.

GETTING OUT

Before getting out of prison, I spent night after night thinking about how I was going to live my life differently. I knew that things needed to change now that I had so many convictions. I'd spent the best years of my life stoned, drunk, on the streets and in detention. It was time to get my shit together.

Instead, I got out of prison and started repeating the same behaviour. Buying the lie that I could just have one hit was crazy. I had proven to myself (and everyone else) that my lifestyle was destroying everything important to me but somehow knowing this was not enough.

I got out and connected straight away with Liam, a guy I had done time with. He hooked me up with half an ounce of heroin and I was straight back to my old habits. I'd already spent all of my workers compensation money and I had parole hanging over my head so my brilliant idea was to sell drugs to support my habit. I seemed to have a death wish.

The selling didn't go too well. I became my own best customer. I ended up burning Liam for the dope and just moved on to others to get credit. I was doing other crimes too, but selling drugs was the main way I survived, if you can call it that.

Misery loves company and, somehow, I convinced Karen to take me back. Karen, Chantelle and I moved in to the garage of my parents' house in Coburg and for me, the only way to cope was to remain stoned. Fucking crazy. The solution to all my problems was in fact my biggest problem.

GETTING OUT

When things got really bad, Karen would take me to see Doctor Jagoda in North Melbourne and either I'd go into detox for a week or get on to a methadone program. Methadone had never really worked for me as a way to get off heroin but it did carry me through until something else came along.

In 1984, Karen became pregnant. While I was medicated to the max, I managed to get a job with my older brother Joe at an electronics factory in Broadmeadows. I started to think my luck had changed so I bought a car and rented a two-bedroom commission flat in Ascot Vale. My new address was Blamey Street - an ironic name for an addict blaming everyone for his issues but himself.

I was burning the wrong people in the underworld. Half an ounce was worth four grand and I owed plenty: getting credit from one bloke, not paying, going to another, not paying. I was constantly in fear, knowing that I could be bashed within an inch of my life, or be killed. With one three-year-old and another baby due to arrive any minute, Karen regretted ever having met me.

On 5 November 1984 Teryn was born in the Royal Women's Hospital. I have no memory of the birth; I probably wasn't even there.

I thought that having a new baby daughter might snap me out of it but sure enough, life got worse. My job was getting difficult to handle and my erratic behaviour came to the attention of the supervisor. I was called to the office with my older brother who was a supervisor in another department. The only thing I could do was admit to being an addict and somehow I managed to keep my job after promising to get back on track. Back to the doctor I went. He increased my dose and things seemed to settle down again. But not for long.

A born-again Christian guy at work took pity on me when I told him about my debts. I took advantage of his good nature and convinced him to loan me $6000. I couldn't believe my luck. The idea was to pay Liam back the $4000 I owed him and Nicky the remaining $2000. I was trying to do the right thing and get out of debt but both dealers took the opportunity to offer me more heroin on credit and, being the addict I was, I accepted. A couple of weeks later I found some other hard-core crims to co-invest (with loaned money) in a large amount of heroin that we planned to sell but of course ended up using ourselves.

Eventually my bad debts caught up with me. I went to score from one of my 'business associates' and instead he came at me with a steel dumbbell to the back of my head. I should have gone to hospital but I just had another hit and headed home. I didn't feel like revealing my bleeding skull to Karen but there was nowhere else to go. I needn't have worried. I arrived at the flat and found a note saying she'd had enough. She'd finally reached her limit. She was taking the kids away somewhere safe. I shouldn't bother looking for them. The car and all our remaining cash was also gone.

I worked my way through my stash without leaving the flat for a couple of days. Finally, I put all my remaining dope in my pocket (it was too valuable to me to leave it behind) and went to the shops. When I came home, the door to the bedroom flew open and two guys I'd never seen before rushed at me with baseball bats screaming, "Where's the gear? Where's the money?" Again, I experienced the agony of being struck on the head.

A neighbour heard the commotion and found me unconscious

on the floor. He called an ambulance. The paramedics strapped me down and took me to the Royal Melbourne Hospital where I was stitched up, bandaged and left in the hallway. As soon as someone mentioned reporting the incident to the police, I was out of there, the remaining dope still in my pocket. I must have looked like death.

With former inmate Kev outside the infamous H Division.
Photo taken before the redevelopment of Pentridge. 1999

Outside B Division.
Pentridge. 1999

PART FOUR – HUNG OUT TO DRY
1984 – 1989

PISTOL & POSSESSION CHARGES

A week after Karen's disappearance she contacted me from a women's refuge. Made a deal, I would straighten up for good if she gave me the car back. She wasn't meant to tell me where the refuge was but she did anyway. Didn't see the kids but I did get the car back.

That same day, my old mate Mario contacted me. He had just been released after doing 12 years in jail. He had some gear and some contacts so I went to pick him up in Brunswick. Mario was with a guy called Ron who I didn't know. The plan was to go and collect some money and take it from there.

We were driving down Racecourse Road when a cop car came around the corner, lights flashing. There were warrants out for my arrest (car fines, breach of parole) and Mario and Ron were fresh out of prison. Not good! The cops pulled in front of us so I had no choice but to pull over. They handcuffed us and searched the car.

It didn't take long for the cops to find a pistol as well as a couple of bags of dope under the back seat. I genuinely had no idea how they got there. They took us to the Flemington police station and started questioning me. I stuck to my story and the others also denied knowing anything. The detectives came in and told me they knew the gun and dope belonged to Mario and Ron; they had seen them raise themselves up and put the stuff under the seat as they were pulling us over. But the car was in my name, I was the driver and I would be the one charged. The others were let go.

I was hung out to dry on serious charges; possession of a pistol alone would guarantee me time in prison. I was well and truly fucked. I made a bail application and sure enough I was granted bail. I couldn't believe it. I was bailed to live at my parents' house – somehow I always ended up there when the shit hit the fan. The family allowed me stay on the condition I did something dramatic to turn around my situation. But I was told not to discuss any of it with them – they didn't want to know the details.

Odyssey House was fast becoming my only option if I wanted to avoid a long jail term. I had truly never wanted to end up there. Odyssey was a rehab with a huge reputation, most of it not pleasant. Long-term bootcamp for people in serious trouble – well I ticked that box! I made a phone call and got all the relevant information. One of the things mentioned during the call was that you could have your kids at Odyssey with you and that a family application would be fast-tracked. My mind went into overdrive.

ODYSSEY HOUSE

I found out that Karen and the kids were now staying with her sister and father in Fawkner. I recruited my younger sister Marie to help arrange for me to see the girls before I went to Odyssey. By then, Teryn was one and Chantelle was nearly four. When I saw Karen, it was clear that she wasn't coping too well financially or emotionally. I convinced myself that the kids would be better off with me at Odyssey.

A few days later, Marie talked Karen into letting me see the kids a second time. I had made a half-hearted effort to wean myself off drugs while living with my family but I had a hit before the scheduled outing. Because I was stoned I had the courage to carry out my plan.

I took the kids to the Odyssey storefront. Effectively I had kidnapped my two daughters. Karen would be beside herself but I told myself that part of her would be relieved to have a break from looking after them both by herself.

I had decided that having the kids with me was the insurance I needed to remain in rehab. Odyssey's policy was that if I wanted to leave, the Department of Human Services would be informed and would probably make the girls wards of the state. Being stoned and desperate, I said Karen's whereabouts were unknown and agreed to the terms.

Chantelle, Teryn and I were processed as in-patients. All of our clothes were searched, we were showered and fed and the kids had their hair checked for lice. That was the easy part. The heroin was wearing off and I started to panic, I had never looked after either of my daughters on my own and I was suddenly overwhelmed. I was told that someone at the house would assess my parenting skills and help me look after the girls. The parents' section was downstairs and the kids were taken upstairs to a toy-filled bedroom. I was told there were a total of 12 kids staying in the program and that someone would be on duty all night watching over them.

I was nervous as fuck. What the hell was I doing there? My head said go and my heart said stay. It was the story of my life - I was always thinking one thing and doing another. I woke up each day to face the consequences of my pathetic actions; my addiction had made me mentally defective.

I went to the lounge room for the evening meeting and met Jimmy, my designated buddy. He was trying to be helpful but I just wanted him to shut up. I was shown around and then taken to my small room and given the run down on what would happen in the morning: 7am wake up, tidy up and then downstairs to take care of my kids. I'd already forgotten they were there. I wanted to go to sleep and not wake up. Instead I lay there wondering how the fuck things had gotten this bad. I felt like a real hypocrite and a complete no-hoper.

In the morning Jimmy came to collect me. I was in no mood for this shit but had to keep reminding myself I had no option - I had to follow through or the kids would end up in welfare and I would either be in prison, on the streets or dead. Seeing the kids was comforting but it was my job to get them ready and feed them and I had no idea what to do. Jimmy turned out to be a godsend; he was a parent in the later stages of the program and he understood what was going on for me.

It was one of the toughest weeks of my life: the kids, withdrawal, wanting to go, knowing I had to stay. I don't think I could have managed without the support of Jimmy and some of the other residents.

I had gone through withdrawal many times but each time seemed like the first. This time was the worst: dry retching, cramps, not being able to eat or sleep, restless and lethargic at the same time.

I was in the pre-treatment group. The first six weeks were an assessment period used to form a treatment plan. With two kids, it was a little more complex and included group therapy sessions, parenting group and some physical work in the kitchen, laundry, garden or office. We were allocated 10 cigarettes a day.

None of this meant anything to me. I was there because my life had spiralled out of control and I was not going to make it. I was going to die of an overdose or be bashed to death and my kids were going to end up in welfare. But the only thing in my mind was getting another shot.

Group therapy sessions were designed to challenge participants about past behaviour. I went to the sessions but my mind was elsewhere. The parenting group was confronting because I was asked about the kids' mother. I just said I didn't know where she was. Occasionally Chantelle also asked about her mother but mostly she and Teryn were distracted by all the activities. The hours turned to days and weeks with no word from Karen.

The withdrawals subsided and I started to feel better physically but mentally, I was fried. My thinking was negative and I wasn't able to express my feelings of rage. I suffered quietly.

COMING CLEAN

A few weeks into the program, Teryn contracted the measles and was rushed to the Austin Hospital. She became very sick and stayed in hospital for two weeks. Thankfully, I was able to visit her daily with a senior staff member from Odyssey. Even when Teryn was critically ill, I didn't contemplate contacting Karen.

I was beginning to surrender to my situation. The urge to run away was slowly diminishing. I was building a bond with the girls and the staff at Odyssey and I felt stronger and more hopeful every day. Luckily, I also knew how to play the game, how to slip by unnoticed most of the time. I had always done well in institutions. In prison I developed an instinct for manipulating the situation in my favour; I worked out ways to get the best food, the easiest jobs and how to be the last one locked up at night. In Odyssey, I knew to keep my opinions to myself and to avoid getting involved with the big personalities around the place. Having the girls with me proved to be a bonus when it came to getting out of household duties and avoiding socialising with the other residents. I would take them for a walk in the garden to get out of washing up and all other non-compulsory sessions. Outward appearances suggested I was doing really well but of course I had a lot of support.

Six weeks into the program, out of the blue, I was called to the office and was served with court papers. Karen was seeking full custody of the children and she had found me through the subpoena process. The papers included a statement from Karen that painted me as a monster. She alleged that I was an unreliable and dishonest drug-addicted criminal who had kidnapped her two small children and was in no way capable of caring for them. All true. But it still cut deep - I was doing all I could to clean myself up.

ODYSSEY HOUSE

Two weeks later, in accordance with the papers, I attended Melbourne Magistrates' Court, supported by Greg representing Odyssey House. Because of the lies I had fed him about Karen's incompetence, he told me that he would be recommending to the court that the girls stay with their father while under treatment. I was feeling nervous and didn't know what to expect. I felt guilty about having put Karen through the pain of not knowing where the kids were or what they were doing, but still hoped the children could remain with me.

At court, Greg asked for a short adjournment so that he could talk in private with Karen. During that session break, Greg convinced her to postpone the custody hearing until I finished the program at Odyssey House. In the meantime, the girls would be returned to her care. I was rocked by this sudden development. I didn't want to lose the girls.

Karen and I were both driven back to the house. The drive took over an hour and neither of us said a word, we were both wondering how the reunion with the kids would play out. I picked them up from the kinder and walked them down the hallway to the foyer where Karen was waiting. Chantelle and Teryn froze when they saw their mum and it took a few minutes for them to warm up to her. Karen was clearly overjoyed to see them. I didn't know how to feel.

RELEGATED

My stay at Odyssey changed dramatically from that moment. My period under supervision and assessment ended and I was given a date for my 'probe', a session during which an individual's life story is probed by a selected group of people consisting of a staff member and four residents from different levels of the treatment program. I was also allowed to bring someone from my peer group in the house. I had never experienced anything like it and I was petrified at the thought of having my history dissected.

The group was given my file and they discussed my case before I was allowed in. At first, they talked to me gently about my life in general but soon enough they started challenging me about my early childhood, the time I had spent in institutions, the drugs and my criminal behaviour. It snowballed and suddenly my whole life was under the microscope. Nothing was left out.

I was defensive and argumentative; I rationalised, denied, justified and minimised. I was sent out of the room a couple of times with my head racing, thinking, fuck this shit! Who do they think they are? Do they know who they are talking to? (Who I thought I was, I don't know.)

I was called back in and told to wait. The door opened and Karen and a support person walked in and sat down. I was told that Karen now had the opportunity to express herself, to confront me about what I had done to her, to the kids, to our life. We stared at each other; then I was torn to shreds for what seemed like ages. She said she had tried to stop me using (which was true). She also made allegations about my drug-fuelled behaviour that I could not recall or refute. I felt betrayed.

Then Karen began crying and was allowed to leave. I was fuming, filled with dark thoughts about the process and all the people who were a party to it. I was asked a few more questions but I couldn't answer, I was ropeable.

It was suggested that I should apologise to Karen. Saying sorry to her was the last thing I felt like doing at that moment but I understood that I had to play along with the process and demonstrate my willingness to make amends for my past actions.

Karen was called back in and I said I was sorry for everything I had put her and the kids through. I knew Karen didn't believe me and I wondered if the group could also recognise that, as far as I had come, I still lacked true remorse. I was still programmed to admit to nothing, to make no concessions.

Karen said she accepted my apology but continued to question my integrity. I repeated my apology and said that I meant what I said. It worked. I was congratulated and told that I had been accepted into the level one 'action' part of the treatment program. I left the room as angry as I'd ever been.

The probe had taken its toll on me and I needed time to regain my equilibrium. The team at Odyssey recommended that I be moved to Sydney Odyssey where I wouldn't be constantly reminded of the girls' absence from the house. After a few days, I begrudgingly agreed to move.

My bail conditions were changed and I was transferred to Sydney. I would be allowed to travel back to Melbourne for regular court dates and to visit the kids. The idea was that once I got over the feeling that I had been fucked over, I could buckle down and swiftly move through the program.

I didn't know anyone in Sydney - no one I had used with or done time with in jail. The distance between my current life and my dark past turned out to be a good thing. I was able to focus on the program and within a couple of months, I had made it to level two. I was doing so well that Karen agreed with Odyssey's suggestion that the kids be flown over to stay with me for a couple of weeks. That time with the kids was a blessing. I was clean and, as inexperienced as I was at being a real dad, they brought me so much happiness that I was able to forget all the pain and suffering. That was the first time I felt like I had some hope, that things might turn out okay for all of us.

I soon made it to level three and was offered the role of program coordinator. I was part of a special peer group that ran the house, answerable only to the level four house supervisor. The role involved a lot of responsibility but I seemed to thrive under the pressure. It had been a long and difficult year but I remained focused on the future. My goal was to reach level four and hopefully become the new house supervisor before my court hearing. I remained committed and kept up the hard work, all the time conscious of the fact that I might end up in prison regardless of all the effort.

My relationships with others in the program developed and I had a few really close friends. In early 1986, I was moved to level four and I was given the role of house supervisor.

My court case was scheduled and arrangements were made for me to fly to Melbourne. I was offered a staff member to accompany me to court but I settled for a reference and a peer. I was picked up at the airport by a resident and taken to the house in Lower Plenty where the kids had been brought to see me. Being with the kids was magical and I was keen to enjoy the day despite the awkwardness with Karen and the knowledge that I could go back to jail.

The next morning I went to the city to meet with my solicitor, Rob, a good guy who was doing a lot of work with people in Odyssey. He was very impressed with the letter and couldn't believe the change in me physically. We agreed that it would be near impossible to defend the charges and we decided I should change my plea to guilty. Rob was positive we had enough ammunition to prove to the court that I was a changed man and that I had a chance at a non-custodial sentence. I was less optimistic but there was nothing more I could do.

My name was called over the speaker at the Melbourne Magistrates' Court. I put out my cigarette and began the walk down the long corridor. Ivan, the senior peer from Odyssey was there to support me. I needed it. The charges were read out and I was asked how I was to plead. Guilty.

For what seemed like hours, Rob made sentencing submissions about my rehabilitation and the fact that I was now a role model to many younger people at Odyssey House in Sydney. The judge asked me to stand up and asked if I had anything to add. I hadn't planned to say anything but found myself saying yes. I said I had learned from my horror past, that addiction was a curse to individuals and society at large, that prison was no answer and finally that if I was given an opportunity I was prepared to face the challenge of life without drugs. I thanked the court and sat back down. You could hear a pin drop.

The magistrate adjourned the case for lunch, which Rob thought was a good sign. For me, the wait was excruciating. After lunch, we all filed back into court. The magistrate finally entered and began his summary. I was asked to stand and he commended me for my hard work and the progress I had made. He assured me that from his time on the bench he understood how difficult it was to break the cycle of addiction but he was convinced my chances were high and he gave me a two-year community based order. If I reoffended or relapsed I would serve that time in prison. I was told to complete the program at Odyssey. I was free to go.

NO HOPER

My time at Odyssey was going on 15 months, my court case was over and my relationships with my children had never been better. I was off the streets and doing well! All seemed great but I still had doubts about my future and my ability to stay clean. I always did well in institutions and I had always been able to convince people that things were okay. Had I just scammed everyone? Was I really a changed man? Unfortunately, my history was my only real reference point.

I decided I was ready to graduate from the program. But my supervisors felt I needed more time. They said that after 15 months they still didn't know anything about me (which I stupidly wore as a badge of honour) and that I needed to move into private one-on-one sessions. Unconsciously I was avoiding that stage of therapy, avoiding the hardest step. I was unwilling to expose my vulnerabilities.

My attitude slowly started to change. I became argumentative, restless, irritable and unhappy. If anyone tried to discuss it with me, I dismissed it as nonsense. I became close to Louise, a level four who had just transferred from New Zealand. We had a lot in common and we started to isolate ourselves from the rest of the peer group, denying that there was anything going on.

I was becoming dishonest, close-minded and unwilling to listen. It was the beginning of my next downfall. Louise and I convinced each other that we could continue our rehabilitation on our own. One day, we decided to abandon the program and while on an outing, we took off.

Initially, leaving Odyssey seemed like a great idea. I believed I had done enough work on myself after 18 months in rehab. But all I had really done was abstain from mood and mind-altering substances for a while.

Louise and I decided to celebrate in a motel room. After a few drinks I went for a walk around Kings Cross. I was out of rehab, I'd had a few, and I was staying in a motel with a gorgeous woman. Suddenly it seemed like a good idea to score some heroin.

The kids in Melbourne, my family, the community based order - none of it seemed important. I was immediately swallowed back into the world I had just managed to escape. I had woken up a monster that had been asleep for 18 months.

Before long our money ran out and our situation deteriorated quickly. Louise thought about working the cross and I considered doing some burglaries. We were scaring the shit out of ourselves. Louise realised she needed to go home to New Zealand. She contacted her family, they sent some money and within a week we tearfully parted ways. I felt bad for the role I had played, for including her in my relapse.

I started to really worry about myself. How was it possible that the threat of a two-year jail term could not deter me from picking up heroin again? With the little money I had left, I scored in Kings Cross and got stoned so that, temporarily at least, I didn't have to think about anything.

My pride and the way I had left the program prevented me from returning to Odyssey. So I decided to contact a few of my siblings and convince them to send me some money to come home. I told them I had completed the program. Every cent I received from them was spent on a cheap bus ticket and enough heroin to see me home.

I walked into one of the laneways where people went to use and I mixed up enough for two hits. I loaded one hit into a syringe and put the cap on for the bus trip. I injected the other hit.

I came to with paramedics all around me. I had overdosed and collapsed in the laneway. Someone had called an ambulance and I was given Narcan and brought back to life. I was furious and frustrated that they had reversed the effects of the heroin (forget about being grateful they had saved my life). In all the commotion, one of the paramedics pricked himself with the loaded syringe I had in my sleeve. He demanded I go back to the hospital to get some blood tests and I told him to get fucked. I walked off down the street, jumped in a cab to the bus depot and waited for the bus to Melbourne.

The effects of the Narcan started to wear off and I was wasted all the way back to Melbourne. Just before arriving, I went to the toilet and had the rest of the heroin in the syringe. It seemed to me that I operated a lot better under the influence of heroin. Despite all the counselling, I continued to buy the lie that I could just use occasionally. Half my head manufactured the bullshit and the other half bought it – every single time.

Four weeks had passed since I had run away from Odyssey. I was running a habit and was in heaps of trouble. I hadn't officially breached my community based order as I hadn't been charged with any offences but I had to quickly come up with a plan. I went to see Doctor Jagoda who had been treating me for addiction for many years, and he convinced me to go on a methadone program and to join the long waiting list to get into rehab.

My family knew I was back so I had no choice. I contacted my mum and some of my brothers and sisters and played the game as best I could. Pretended to be just fine. I even convinced my elder sister Annette to let me live with her and her four daughters in Glenroy. Outwardly I still looked okay but inwardly I was falling apart.

Karen was living with the children in Templestowe. She had been told that I'd left the program and, with the support of Melbourne Odyssey, was refusing to allow me access to the kids. If I wanted to see Chantelle and Teryn I would need a urine test to prove I was clean. I came unstuck. I attempted to see the kids by turning up at their preschool but the police were called so I had to split.

The methadone program wasn't stopping me from using and my life continued to deteriorate. My family was becoming aware of my lifestyle again and my sister was concerned about me using while living in her house.

Somehow the weeks turned to months and, miraculously, I made it through my two-year order without being charged. I no longer had the threat of prison hanging over my head.

I couldn't accept that I wasn't allowed to see the kids but instead of doing something about my habit, I spat the dummy and blamed Karen for everything. I told myself that not seeing the kids was the reason I was out of control. The truth was Karen was doing a great job looking after herself and the girls, better than I ever could.

At nearly 30, I was back living in my mum's garage, selling drugs and committing other crimes. I overdosed regularly; brought back

NO HOPER

to life only to continue to trash it. My mum was always waiting for the knock on the door to be told that I had died.

My brothers loathed me; my sisters felt pity for me; my dad was disgusted; and my mum tried to love me. But finally even she had had enough and I was told the garage was no longer available to me. One of my brothers told me to go away and die somewhere and leave the family alone.

My doctor increased my dose of methadone and apart from that, there was nothing more that could be done for me. I was helpless and hopeless.

With Teryn. 1988

Teryn and Chantelle.
A day at the zoo. 1989

With Teryn and Chantelle. Chantelle's ninth birthday.

PART FIVE – RECOVERY
1989

PLEASANT VIEW

My first attempts at recovery were full of desperation, degradation, homelessness, moving in and out of institutions, and relapsing into old habits of drug and alcohol abuse. Believing I had failed in all areas of my life - including as a son, brother, partner and most of all as a father - I truly believed I had nothing to offer, and had no real hope that I could change my life.

In 1989, I was finally admitted to Pleasant View Drug and Alcohol Facility in Wood Street, Preston. I was still on the replacement drug, methadone. I had been on and off 'the done', a synthetic opiate, for years. I used it so I wouldn't hang out. It was supposed to stop me from craving heroin but I had built such a tolerance that it never mattered how much methadone I was on, I continued to use heroin and anything else I could get and never seemed to be satisfied.

The staff at Pleasant View knew me on a first name basis, as I had been an inpatient and outpatient on numerous occasions. Marion called me into the office with my file in front of her, and it was fucking huge.

Marion: "Welcome back Leonard, I hope you give it your best shot."

Me: "Of course, why else do you think I'm here?"

Marion: "Well, based on your file, you have had numerous admissions and have never had a clean urine. So what's different this time?"

Me: "I don't know." (For once I didn't have an answer.)

Marion: "I have never heard that from you before - that you don't know. Maybe there is hope for you yet."

And so my detox began. I was attempting to come off all drugs. The doctor was initially dubious about my ability to come off methadone, so the plan was to reduce the dose by 2.5 milliliters a day. I was on 60 so it was going to take a while. I was prescribed all sorts of pills, from sleepers to vitamins.

The first week was not too bad but from then on I started to feel the withdrawal. Not too sure if most of the feelings were real or imagined. Didn't notice much about anything - the staff, other patients. All I knew was there was something different about my attitude. The cramps and the sweats were just some of the sensations I started to feel. The longer I went without using, and the more I reduced the methadone, the more I felt emotionally. I had never coped properly with strong feelings.

I recall one particular group meeting that in many ways was a turning point in my motivation to get clean. We were asked a series of questions about how we would like to live our life if no obstacles stood in our way. I volunteered to come up to the front and have my answers written on the board:

Where would you like to live? A farm house overlooking the water.

What would you like to do for a living? Work for myself, helping other people.

What wage would you be satisfied with? $100k per year.

Would you like to travel? Yes to Italy, London, Amsterdam, Bangkok and New Zealand.

What car would you like to own? A Maserati Quattroporte.

How clean and sober would you like to be? One year clean.

What sort of traits would you like to have? I would like to be honest, loyal, trustworthy, reliable, a role model.

How would you like your relationship with your kids to be? Trusting, loving, respectful and responsible.

Relationship with your family? Supportive, loving, respectful, trusting.

Friends? Loyal, trustworthy, reliable, supportive and genuine.

Finally, describe the woman of your dreams. Gorgeous, smart, loyal, loving, successful, fit, supportive.

We had a short break before we were asked to compare our answers to our current reality.

Where do you live? In a drug rehab for addicts.

What do you do for a living? I am unemployable and on the dole.

What sort of car do you own? I have no car and no license.

Are you clean and sober? No, I am on methadone and detoxing.

Where have you travelled? From jail to jail in a meat wagon.

What traits do you have? I am dishonest, untrustworthy, unreliable, a fucking disgrace.

Relationship with children and family? No contact, no trust, irresponsible, shameful.

Friends? Only drug users and people like myself.

A description of your partner? No partner.

Then we were all asked one more question: If we wanted all the things on the first lot of questions, why were we settling for the shit that was our real life? I had been to many detoxes, rehabilitation and counselling sessions but I had never previously seen my life as it really was - a total mess. I was putting in an order for my life, but not doing anything to make it a reality. It suddenly all made sense to me and at that moment I decided to do whatever I had to, to get clean.

After three weeks, most of the illegal drugs were out of my system and whatever methadone I was on, wasn't holding me. The real detox began. The methadone was being given to me at the clinic and the doctors decided that the dose would be a dummy dose, which meant I didn't know the amount. I started to feel really sick and the doctor was called a few times but the majority of time, all they wanted to do was prescribe more pills. For the first time in my life, I told the doctor no more pills, no more medication of any sort. By this time, the methadone was down to only a few milliliters.

The staff extended my stay a few times because I was so sick; I was trying to eat but couldn't and my restlessness was out of control. I couldn't sleep and at times I was even accused of using speed as I would stay up all night. I had to give supervised urine samples and, because I hadn't used, I knew they would come back clean. But things were not getting better for me. I didn't have any contact with my kids, family, or anyone for that matter. My world consisted of the facility and the people involved; patients would come and stay for hours, days or weeks, and a rare few would complete the program. I didn't know much about what was going on, I had never been through anything like it before and it only seemed to get worse. Some of the staff finally started to believe that I was seriously attempting to end my dependence on drugs. Patients would use and I wasn't involved; some would leave but I stayed.

PLEASANT VIEW

The weeks turned into months and I started attending meetings of AA and NA. I really didn't understand what was going on there, I was just trying to get out of the ward and the meetings were an outlet. I made a friend named Phil who was similar to me; our backgrounds were jails, institutions and the streets. We started attending meetings together and, at one particular meeting, we made contact with members of an agency called the US Society - Understanding and Support; an organisation that supplied supported accommodation for people who were newly clean. Phil and I both put our names on the list to join the society and rang daily to check our progress up the list.

The meetings were really beginning to help. Hearing the stories of people who had stopped using gave me some hope but, at times, I truly believed I didn't deserve anything good. Some of those I met appeared happy and seemed to be enjoying their lives, so I kept going; attending with Phil really helped as I didn't feel alone.

My stay at Pleasant View was coming to an end and my commitment to getting into the US Society paid off when both Phil and I were called into the office to be told we had been accepted. We would be moving within a few days. It had been over six weeks and all drugs were now out of my system. The only frustrating thing was that sleep was still eluding me and, no matter how active I was during the day, I never seemed to be tired enough to sleep. Other members of the US Society would tell me to keep going and that things would get better.

My life had never been this good. I was finally able to identify as clean - really clean - and as overwhelmed as I was, life actually seemed to be going well.

US SOCIETY

A couple of members from the US Society came and picked Phil and me up from Pleasant View. Leaving somewhere that I had felt so safe and supported for the first time in my life was really sad and quite scary. But it was time to put the lessons I had learnt from all of my failed attempts to get clean, into action. I was a member of the US Society; I was attending the meetings; and I was accepted as someone worthy. It felt good, very good.

In March 1990, I moved into a US Society house in Grange Road, Ormond with Phil and two other members, Debbie and Tracy who were ahead of me in the program.

The US Society drop-in centre was in Chapel Street, St Kilda where groups were held twice a week. Check-ins and attendance at meetings was compulsory. I believed I could manage, with the support of Phil, and other members attending the meetings. John, the manager was also very supportive.

The first week in the house in Ormond, I stayed up most nights cleaning the place from top to bottom. My sleepless nights were very annoying for everyone; most people thought I was using but my urine kept coming back clean. Eventually I started to sleep for a few hours here and there and life was continually surprising me so I just kept going.

One Thursday group day in Chapel Street, Phil and I were standing out the front talking to a few others when Phil called me aside to tell me he was going. I asked where and he said he'd had enough and couldn't do it anymore. I was taken aback and attempted to talk him out of it but no matter what I said, he had already made up his mind. Phil thanked me for being a true friend and just walked off. I remember standing there waiting for him to realise what a mistake he was making and turn around and come back. That didn't happen. I kept watching him walk away until he disappeared into the distance. A very sad day indeed. My recovery buddy had deserted me and I was on my own.

The other people in the house also moved on; no one seemed to stay for long. I knew I had nowhere to go, so I stayed and just kept going to meetings.

Part of the deal was that once settled, you would move to a three-quarter way house. So I moved from Grange Road to Osborne Street, South Yarra, a couple of houses from Toorak Road. I settled in with my new housemates Shelly, Andrea and Marianne and life seemed to be going my way. I had been clean from all drugs for quite a while and even though I felt really raw and at times numb, I had become one of the senior residents with some say in the house. However, people didn't seem to hang around. I would get really close to someone only to watch them either leave or relapse. In most cases, people left to go use. It is what I had been doing all my life and, for a change, it wasn't me. At one point, for a nine-month period I was living in that house on my own.

I became really close to a few females and I realised that I had never been with anyone while clean. Sex became another addiction. It made me feel good and I couldn't get enough. I just wanted more and more and this became a huge issue. The rationale I used was that at least I wasn't using drugs. I talked openly about the issue to friends and members of the US Society and received different advice from, "Just don't use" to "I wish I had that problem" and the occasional "You need to take a good look at that." As far as I was concerned, my new problem really didn't compare to jails, institutions and overdoses.

My elder brother helped me get a $10 grand loan that I used to pay off all my fines and a couple of other debts. I bought myself a 240K Datsun Coupe. My first job in recovery was as a labourer for one of my housemate's dad, Allan, who was the CEO of a building company. The money was good and I paid off my loan.

According to the house rules, I had to continue to attend meetings during the day so at lunch time I would make an appearance at the midday meeting in Lonsdale Street in the city and then quickly leave and go back to work. So I was working, attending meetings, keeping up my responsibilities to the US Society, and I still had time to indulge my new addiction.

I was finally a part of something. I was invited to dinners, barbecues, people's homes. I was working closely with both men and women. I was trusted by some, held in high regard by others. Some even considered me to be special. Sometimes I bought into the bullshit and my ego grew so big that it was difficult to reconcile with my innate feelings of low self-esteem.

MEETING SUE

A mate and supportive US Society member called Richard introduced me to Sue. She touched my cheek and said what beautiful skin I had. I remember it clearly; no one had ever touched me like that. I joked with a friend that she could sponsor me any day.

A few weeks later, Sue asked if I could give her a lift to Geelong to drop off a CV for a job she was going for. We made a night of it; Sue, myself and a friend called Donald went to Geelong, did a meeting, dropped off the CV, laughed and had a great time.

Sue told me she had a stall at the South Melbourne Market that weekend so I dropped in to visit her and she was pleased to see me. Sue was blond and gorgeous. She was an articulate and intelligent school teacher. I didn't think I had a chance. She had been in recovery for a few years and would probably want to be with someone with a better track record.

That night, Sue and I went out and everything seemed to go smoothly. But my reputation with women did come up. Was I having unprotected sex? Things I had never discussed with anyone. I had been talking with a sponsor about it but it had never been a real issue before because I was single and not attached to anyone. I was always advised by my sponsor to 'check my motives'. What that meant I wasn't sure but I agreed to try.

Our connection grew and a relationship developed. I had never had a relationship while I was clean so I was acting as if I knew what I was doing but really I was bluffing my way. The sex was insane, the time we spent together was bliss and my attention to other women seemed to subside. My only focus was Sue. I was learning heaps about life and clean relationships.

My job was going well and my attendance at meetings was consistent, I was working closely with a sponsor and I was now the senior resident at the US Society. I was dining at the best cafes in Toorak (which seemed to suit me well) and I started staying over at Sue's place some nights.

I also started reconnecting with my kids, Chantelle and Teryn who were living with Karen in Reservoir. Every Monday, Wednesday and Friday I would drive from South Yarra to Reservoir, pick the girls up and take them to school. I also made an effort to see them every weekend. They would come with me to meetings and play with the other kids or we would go and visit my mum. Making amends and acting responsibly was part of my recovery but mostly I did it so that I could spend as much time with them as possible. They brought immense joy to my life.

My sponsor was challenging me to accept and even sometimes understand some of what had happened and have some faith that all would end up okay. I was constantly drilled that I must remain honest, open-minded and willing, and only then would I have a chance to truly turn my life around. It wasn't easy as I had been dishonest, close-minded and unwilling for most of my life. But I kept up the hard work.

The chaos of my old life had disappeared, replaced with this new reality. At times it felt like a dream, I really had to pinch myself. From jails, institutions, overdoses, broken relationships, priors as long as my arm… How I had lived to tell the tale was beyond

MEETING SUE

me. But it was my tale and it had people talking. I had become really close to some people through the recovery process and new possibilities were taking shape.

INTERVIEWS

After a meeting one night, Tony - a guy from the Salvation Army who I really looked up to - sat me down with a couple of US Society members.

He opened the conversation by asking whether I had ever thought about working in the field of drug and alcohol rehabilitation. I thought he was taking the piss - I mean I could hardly read or write and had left school at the age of 14 (without passing year seven). I couldn't believe they were asking *me* to consider helping *other* people. They told me they believed I had a lot to offer people who were coming into recovery, which was news to me!

Apparently two part-time positions were becoming available: one as support worker at the US Society, and the other as an outreach worker for the St Kilda Community Health Centre (CHC). They suggested I apply for both jobs, each requiring a commitment of 20 hours a week. I thought it was a complete waste of time, but Tony strongly encouraged me to apply for the jobs. I felt I was being pushed somewhere I had never been and didn't belong.

I asked Tony, "What am I supposed to put in my résumé - all my detoxes and the jails and institutions I have been in?" His answer blew me away. "Leonard, your past, your experience, your strength and your courage to carry on is without parallel. I will help you put together a resume that demonstrates that you are an experienced and professional applicant for both jobs."

The first interview was at the St Kilda CHC. The job involved working on the streets of St Kilda to provide outreach to people

INTERVIEWS

living rough and/or struggling with substance abuse, to educate people on safe using procedures and safe sex practices. Really, all my experience had been exactly the opposite – using drugs dangerously and having unprotected sex. The interview lasted 20 minutes, although it seemed an eternity, and I was told that they would get back to me. I took that to mean, thanks but no thanks.

The interview for the US Society was a little different as I knew most of the people on the panel. However there were a number of quality applicants so I thought it would be nothing more than good practice at being interviewed. The job consisted of providing intensive support for people trying to access the agency and to also offer support to those in the agency. Having been through the process myself - and still at the time a participant - I was easily able to articulate my responses to their questions. The interview ended and, once again, I was told they would ring me back.

I woke up one day and started on my regular morning activities – cleaning, the daily readings, meditating - when the phone rang. It was the St Kilda CHC.

"Hello, is Leonard there?"

"Leonard speaking, how can I help?"

"Cathy here. Congratulations, you were successful in your application and we would like to offer you the job. When can you start?"

I hung up the phone stunned, shocked; I had to sit down. Just as I sat, the phone rang again.

"Hello, is Leonard there?"

"Leonard speaking."

"It's John here from US Society. Congratulations on your

application; you got the job. When can you come in for a chat?"

As I hung up the phone, I really couldn't believe what had just happened. Having had no belief in my chances of getting either job and then being successful in both, the joy was overwhelming. My feelings were too strong to handle. I started to shake and I put my head in my hands and then let out a huge scream; some of the others came out of their rooms to see what the fuss was about. Shelley, Andrea and Marian all asked at the same time what had happened. Everyone seemed to be genuinely happy for me but the thing that surprised me the most was that everyone had believed I would get both jobs – everyone that is, except me.

WORKING LIFE

Before beginning my two new jobs I had to move out of my current residence; there was a conflict of interest now that the US Society, which owned the house, had become my employer. I found a pleasant little two-bedroom flat in Marine Parade, St Kilda, and moved in with a new flat mate, Ken. He was often away and was cleaner than me - it worked out perfectly. I was also getting on really well with Sue and our relationship was becoming serious.

The outreach job in St Kilda was four nights a week from Thursday to Sunday from 8pm until 2am. The team would usually start by meeting at the Mitford Street CHC to talk about the night ahead. Then we would go out on the streets to engage with drug users, working girls and boys, and criminals. I loved the work; I was in my element working on the streets, helping drug users, and the nightlife that came with it. In my other job at the US Society, I worked Wednesday to Friday from 10am till 4pm. The two jobs worked beautifully together, the money was good and the conditions great.

It didn't take long before our outreach team became known to the users and the working girls and boys. Sometimes we just handed out using kits and condoms. Other times we would spend hours talking to people about recovery, detox and rehabilitation centers, and meetings. Because of my own experiences, I was able to communicate with people who wouldn't listen to anyone else. I could provide support to people that everyone else had given up on. People were inspired by me and it was the job of my dreams, but it also directly exposed me to a way of life that I had spent a long time and a great effort trying to leave behind. Late at night there were always incidents, from working girls getting raped to drug users overdosing. My recovery had not been seriously challenged until I started that job and it was becoming a struggle; my old and new life were starting to collide.

The job at the US Society was very different. The focus was on recovery, being aware of triggers, staying out of old environments (which was ironic given my outreach job) and remaining committed to the process. Group meetings, one-on-one counselling and then reporting to John the manager for supervision. I was counselled and held accountable for how I was going with my own recovery and how I was handling my new responsibilities.

Months turned into a year and Sue and I moved in together in Kingsville. I enjoyed going home to Sue and the new life we had created but I still felt like a bit of a fraud in the relationship; I was more comfortable at work spending time with 'my own' people.

My job at the US Society was keeping me sane while my job on the St Kilda streets was starting to expose some of my vulnerabilities. My nights were getting longer; I developed friendships with people who were using; flirted with some of the working girls. Boundaries went out the window. My life started to suffer in all areas.

With my daughters Chantelle and Teryn. Before getting clean. 1989

PART SIX - WAKING THE MONSTER
1990 - 2003

INJURY

My relationship with Sue was really struggling. We were always fighting so we decided to have a break. I left and moved into a house in Douglas Parade, Williamstown with a friend from US Society called Gary. He was a seaman who went out to sea for six weeks at a time, so that suited me fine.

In the meantime I continued to work at the US Society and St Kilda CHC, and regularly attended meetings. I also joined a recovery basketball team with Lee and Nick that played on Monday nights at Elwood College. I was still very good at basketball and found it a great outlet. I played like my life depended upon it and the team became very competitive.

One day my sponsor Michael came to watch me play in a game against the second team in the competition. We were leading by a few points; I stole the ball and was attempting a layup when an opponent tried to block me. He hit me on the side on my left leg and then fell on top of me. I heard a crack in my knee and knew I had done some damage. The game stopped as I was carried off; later I tried to go back on the court but collapsed. We lost the game and I was fucking spewing. The pain was excruciating and Michael offered to drive me to the hospital but I thought it could wait until the morning. However the pain got worse so I rang a doctor who came to the house. He checked my knee and told me I needed X-rays and to see a specialist. Then he offered me something for the pain - and gave me an injection of morphine.

The familiar sensation of feeling completely and comfortably numb washed over me and I forgot all about my knee and the pain. I justified to myself that it was different this time - a doctor had given the drug to me for a valid reason. However the experience was all too familiar: the recovery, all the hard work, the friends I'd made, my two beautiful children – all seemed to vanish in a second.

The next day the doctor at the hospital in Williamstown told me I needed a knee reconstruction and would require a brace. I was prescribed pure codeine phosphate tablets and my relapse began. I was given a week off work and had a few visits from close friends including Michael, Tony, and Nick.

I was so sedated and relieved of the pain in my knee that I felt like superman. Tony asked what I was on and warned me to be careful. I knew what he meant but pretended that I was in control of the situation. After a week I had finished all the tablets and was on a waiting list for surgery. I started to crave more pills, or morphine - anything.

I had woken the monster that had taken me so many years to put to sleep. I was petrified. I returned to meetings white-knuckled and desperately trying to act like I was okay. This was the moment I was supposed to ring my sponsor and ask for help. But instead I pretended I could manage my feelings alone and hoped that the cravings would just go away. They didn't.

BECOMING A FATHER AGAIN

I loved Sue so much and I moved back in but I was unable to make the love work. Sue accused me of being unsupportive. The truth was that I didn't know how to be in a functioning relationship and I didn't really believe I deserved to be happy. I was terrified of commitment and had no real experience at being a loving partner when sober, but we kept trying.

After some time, Sue became pregnant and Dean Vincent McDonald Ottone was born on 13 April 1991. Naming our beautiful son Dean was something Sue and I decided together.

The birth of my son was overwhelming and yes, tears of joy and all the rest, but there was something missing and I didn't know what it was. My time with Dean was as special to me as air itself but it was not enough as my relationship with Sue was suffering: arguments, dishonesty and all the other difficulties were reappearing. And, as I had done most of my life, I just wanted to run. Where to I didn't know. Just away.

I was spending more time at work than at home. My love for my son was killing me because I didn't know what to do. Even the love I had for my older girls seemed to be only in my mind. My actions seemed to demonstrate that the only person important to me, was myself. Knowing this (but not being able to change it) was, at times, excruciating.

I remembered my mum saying that if I really loved my kids, I wouldn't be behaving the way I was. I understood it at the time because I was out there using, in prisons etc. But when Dean was born I wasn't using, I was attempting to lead a respectable life, and I still felt out of my league.

Still, my time with Dean was special. Taking him for walks to the park, holding him, feeding him… almost helped me feel normal. Almost.

ST KILDA STREETS

The job on the streets of St Kilda was becoming increasingly challenging. I had become too involved in the lives of some of the people I was working with on the streets. Raff, a very good friend, overdosed one night after spending most of the evening with me and that affected me in a huge way. Then Kim, one of the working girls, became obsessed with me. She had a reputation as a very tough girl you didn't fuck with and she was working to support a huge drug habit. Kim started talking to me about getting clean and began coming to meetings, but she somehow thought that I was part of the recovery package. I was trying to get back with Sue so it became a little awkward.

One night, I was walking down Fitzroy Street and Kim yelled out to me and started walking towards me. As she got closer, she grabbed me and shoved a brown paper bag down my jumper. She told me not to look at it, that she wanted me to have it so she wouldn't spend it all on heroin. The bag was full of 50 dollar notes: a total of seven grand. Kim had ripped off a mug (customer) as he was about to have a shower before sex. She had gone through his wallet, taken all his money and run off. That was her life.

I kept the stolen money, which was a mistake. Where would I draw the line? I knew I had to choose one way of life or the other, but I would justify my actions by thinking that at least I wasn't using.

After that, Kim continued to give me money. She saw me as a saviour of some sort and she was trying to impress me. She was succeeding. She had a few sugar daddies who would let her drive their BMWs and Mercs and give her cash which she would, in turn, give to me. This continued for a while until eventually Kim got locked up for a serious crime.

I only really felt accepted when I was hanging out on the streets of St Kilda with 'my type' of people. It was a relief. I really only felt okay when others needed me. I was working on the same streets I had hung out on when using drugs in the past, visiting the same jails I had been locked up in, and mixing with people who'd had the same struggles that I was attempting to overcome. I couldn't see that working in this environment was damaging my own attempts to live in a healthy and balanced way because I was finally getting the attention and affirmation that I had missed out on for much of my life.

My friends and family started to notice a change in my behaviour. They became concerned and advised me to stop working in that particular job. I knew they were right but I refused to slow down, let alone stop. I had no self-esteem but I had a huge ego that needed to be fed; I thought I was invincible.

As fearful as I was of using again, my actions did eventually lead me back to drugs. I felt overqualified to go back to meetings but I went anyway. I started sitting in the front row, which was considered intensive care. The sole purpose of the meetings was to share as, 'a problem shared is a problem halved'. However I wouldn't share as I didn't want people to know what was going on and I was becoming as sick as my secrets. John the manager could be very helpful but I was selective about what I revealed to him. And I only spoke to my sponsor on a superficial level. No one really knew what it entailed to sponsor someone like me, partly because I'd been an addict for such a long time.

If I'd bothered to pick up the phone, I would have rung Gary, my mentor and close friend but he was away at sea. I wasn't good at asking for help. That was always hard for me. So was saying, 'sorry' or, 'I love you'.

Attention from women helped. So did going to the gym. But all of these factors could only satisfy me so far. I always seemed to feel the same void; I never felt fulfilled. The more I had, the more I wanted. The more I got, the less I coped.

Sue and I were on and off again. It was a love-hate relationship; when I was away, I wanted to be with her and Dean but when I was there, I wanted to be as far away as possible.

MY FOURTH CHILD

The most beautiful little girl ever, my fourth child, Michaela McDonald Ottone was born on 15 February 1993 at the Royal Melbourne Hospital in Carlton. Sister of Dean, step-sister of Chantelle and Teryn, daughter of Sue McDonald and Leonard Ottone.

I was there to support Sue through the labour - which seemed to go on forever - and the difficult birth. Sue was exhausted; my daughter didn't seem to want to come out into the world that awaited her.

I felt so much love for my family, but also anguish and confusion as my relationship with Sue further deteriorated; I was unable to express – or even understand – my own feelings. I wanted to fix our relationship but it seemed to be heading nowhere. My inability to connect as a father, a partner and a human being showed just how damaged I was and how much work I needed to do. I just didn't know how to be a loving partner.

We argued and either I would threaten to leave or Sue would ask me to go. My suffering was intense as I really wanted to stay and work things out, but my pride and stubborn nature prevailed and I would say, fuck this, I'm out of here.

BELIEVING THE BULLSHIT

After I got clean (again), I decided to leave my two jobs and I got a new job with Brosnan Services. My role at Brosnan was to support young people as they transitioned from prisons and youth training centers by helping them to find housing and jobs.

I was invited to attend meetings at the rehabilitation centers Windana, Odyssey House, Moreland Hall and other institutions. I even started attending meetings at Turana Youth Training Centre and then in K Division, the drug unit in Pentridge Prison. At first I couldn't get clearance to enter some of the prisons due to my prior convictions, however eventually I was given permission to enter in a professional capacity.

Weekly meetings at Malmsbury Youth Training Centre were particularly rewarding. Kelvin, who also worked at Brosnan, would accompany me and we would drive together for over an hour to the facility in a company car. One of the workers, Roger would greet us and would often sit in on the meetings that we ran with groups of young men.

The purpose of the meetings was to demonstrate that the cycle of using drugs and incarceration could be broken and that life offered other opportunities. Kelvin would begin by telling his life story and his experiences with drugs and crime. At first the young men would be suspicious but also curious; when I followed up with my own similar story, some would open up and start to ask questions. Many of those young men really wanted to change their life but didn't know how to ask for help or really understand how to take the first steps.

Kelvin and I attended every week; the group grew from about six to 20 young men and we all got to know each other very well. Some were eventually released from Malmsbury to Brosnan Youth Services, and because we had built a rapport with them, their recovery process had already begun.

The work was fulfilling however I suspected many of the young people were reoffending and that the agency could do a lot more. I began taking young people with me to do talks in institutions and connected them to other agencies such as Rec Link, which organised competitions in basketball, football, indoor cricket and other outings.

The feedback from staff at the prisons and youth training centres was always positive and constructive and at times we would also receive letters of thanks from young men we had helped. This feedback was rewarding and at times I felt truly blessed that I was finally able to make sense of my past and that something positive had come from my very destructive life.

I continued attending meetings for a number of years with various colleagues. At one stage I heard that Kelvin had relapsed and was missing in action; the reality was that we were all recovering and from time to time one of the people I was working with would relapse or disappear. Some overdosed, and a few were even murdered – that was the life I had come to know and understand.

In 1994 I was presented with the Michael Davies Memorial Award for outstanding services in the care and resettlement of offenders. It was a very overwhelming moment. Some people put me on a pedestal, which was fine except that I started to believe my own bullshit. All I had really done was get clean and take up a few opportunities that had come my way.

RED CARPET

In early 1995, the Australian Broadcasting Corporation (ABC) contacted Bernie Geary, the manager at the Brosnan Centre. They were producing a mini-series about life in prison, drug addiction and the welfare system and wanted to hear from a youth worker, an ex-addict and a former prisoner to ensure the series was authentic. Bernie Geary thought he'd keep it simple and send just me along; I ticked all the boxes.

I met with a team of writers, editors and actors and told my story from the beginning. I spoke about my experiences in the juvenile justice system, my decades of drug and alcohol abuse, living on the streets, my progression into the adult prison system. I spoke about emerging from the chaos and my journey into recovery.

Afterwards I was approached by Arianna Bosi, a script editor at the ABC. She thanked me for giving such an honest and compelling account of my life and asked if I would be interested in being an advisor on the set of *Corelli*. She wanted me to spend time with Hugh Jackman who was to play a prisoner and Deborra-Lee Furness who had the role of a single mum and psychologist working in the prison system. I'd never heard of either of them.

Over the next few months, I took Hugh on a tour of the Brosnan Centre and to the Odyssey House storefront in Prahran; we spent time just walking around, having coffee and talking about life in prison. Hugh was good company, a genuinely lovely guy, humble and sincere despite all the attention he received everywhere we went.

RED CARPET

The series was shot over four months at locations all over Melbourne and the old prison in Geelong. It felt like a full circle moment when I was picked up by a limousine in Carlton and driven to prison in Geelong to spend time with Hugh, Deborra-Lee and the other actors.

On set, my opinion was respected and I was asked for guidance throughout. My experience was especially appreciated when the actors needed to prepare a hit of heroin.

The series was launched at a red carpet formal dinner at the Old Melbourne Gaol. I had my photo taken with Hugh and Deborra-Lee, we laughed and ate. I felt good about my contribution and was proud to have my name in the credits at the end of each of the episodes. I was later happy to find out that Hugh and Deborra-Lee, who had met while filming the series, had fallen in love and married.

BURNT OUT

In 1996 I helped to set up another program, Connexions through Jesuit Social Services, which also ran Brosnan Youth Services. The program was designed to provide support for people getting out of jail or off drugs. This opportunity gave my life new focus; I continued attending meetings but also spent more time supporting youths in hospitals and institutions. From our office in Langridge Street, Collingwood we spent many hours on the phone, trying to get people into detox and rehabilitation programs and emergency accommodation, and assessed others for suitability for our housing programs.

The work was hectic and stressful but also rewarding. Connexions was very successful at times, and we received many letters of gratitude and gestures of appreciation from people whose lives had been turned around. However most of the programs were pilot programs funded for one or two years before being closed due to a change of government or health policy or lack of funding, which became increasingly frustrating.

I continued to spend a lot of time attending the meetings in K Division at Pentridge; I had been in jail with some of the men I was now supporting and the meetings became more and more popular. I felt really important which distracted me from dealing with my own issues and my own need for support.

At times it seemed that my life was crazier now than it had been in the past when I was using drugs and had an excuse for being out of control. I was replacing one crazy addiction with another:

working and helping others. I started seeing a psychiatrist, Bill McLeod in Ascot Vale once a week. On one hand I was being told how great I was doing by the people I worked with, and those I was supporting, and on the other hand I felt confused, lost and alone.

I was burnt out but the only thing I could do was keep going; I started to do more and more until at times I became manic. The time I spent on my own was uncomfortable and I was stressed and depleted when I was with my kids. My problem had something to do with facing who I really was, rather than defining myself simply by what I did… so I just kept going.

As I was attending an 'abstinence program', any single drink, pill or joint is considered a relapse. Whereas 'harm minimisation programs' consider using a drug just once a lapse, only continuous use is considered a relapse. Harm minimisation programs are based on the philosophy that it is too hard to stop using every type of alcohol or drug completely so it allows moderate use of less harmful drugs after the completion of the program. The goals are the same — reducing the damaging effects of alcohol and drugs — but the approaches are different. My history had proven that, for me, abstinence is the only effective pathway to recovery.

Unfortunately, I started using heroin again in my time off - a relapse according to any definition. So I booked myself into Windana for a week. In a weird way, relapsing felt like a relief as, all of a sudden, the work stopped, I was no longer supporting all those people, and I no longer had to live up to the expectations of the people who had put me on a pedestal.

I took some time off before returning to the prisons and institutions, but nothing really significant changed in my work life.

I would go to meetings and share my experiences; hope was all I had and was all I could offer. I chose to believe that as long as I told the truth things would work out.

Most people knew that I had relapsed and many respected the fact I was able to bounce back; but I also had my critics who had other opinions about me. They could see that I wasn't really dealing with my underlying issues: my lack of self-esteem, the shame and guilt of my criminal background, denial of the power of my addiction.

In 1998, I was excited to be offered the opportunity to work at the Youth Substance Abuse Service (YSAS), believing I had a lot to contribute. However, I quickly became very frustrated and disappointed in the new job. I spent many hours stuck in meeting after meeting, listening to people talking - mostly psycho-babble. I tried to spend as much time as possible out of the office doing the work I do best: helping people in the grips of addiction. Smith Street, Collingwood - where I had begun my own journey of crime and addiction - became my new work place.

Due to my work at Connexions, I knew most of the users in Smith Street as well as the surrounding suburbs and the commission flats. The young people we worked with needed all sorts of support, from detoxing to long-term supported accommodation, counselling, long-term rehabilitation, and access to drop-in centers.

The government fully funded YSAS so access to money was not an issue. However, to me, the main problem was that once a troubled youth turned a certain age they no longer had access to many services; they moved into the adult system which was dramatically different. But no one took any notice of my ideas - I was just a recovering drug addict. You needed to be mates with someone important or in a high-powered job to be taken seriously. Bobby Dunne, a social worker, once said to me, "Leonard, all you have to do is clock on, do a day's work and clock off." It was great advice but not very easy for me to follow.

I was working with teenagers as young as 13. It was difficult because we had to report these kids to human services and often wait for permission to get them into detox, rehabilitation or access to replacement drugs. By the time human services responded it was often too late to provide the help they needed. Besides, I had a rapport with these teenagers and they respected and trusted me and I knew they were afraid of being reported to human services. During this time I continued to go to meetings in Coburg - held next to my old home, Pentridge Prison - every Thursday night.

After many years of conflict and tension, my relationship with Sue finally ended for good. She met someone else and I was devastated. We went our separate ways but I was determined to see the kids regularly and made that a priority.

NAOMI

I soon met a young woman who I thought was absolutely gorgeous. Naomi and I developed a friendship and for three months we regularly met up for coffee, lunch, dinner or a movie. Finally our relationship progressed and after some time she moved into my place in Roberts Street, West Footscray.

One night I met her father at an Italian restaurant in South Yarra and we talked for ages. He and Naomi's mum had some initial concerns about our age difference - I was 38 while she was only 21 - but he appeared genuinely pleased about our relationship and the fact that Naomi was so happy.

I was in love in a way I had never experienced before, we supported each other and had a number of things in common including a love of basketball. Eventually I met the rest of Naomi's family and she spent some time with my kids and all seemed to go okay. We made a plan: if we were still together in five years we would get married. I had never discussed plans with anyone previously; in the past when I met someone, we would get together, my partner would fall pregnant, we'd have kids and the relationship would slowly sour.

After a while, the house next door to us in Roberts Street came on the market. It was passed in at auction so I approached the owner with an offer and he accepted. I felt very proud to have purchased the property, I was achieving something and participating in society in a healthy way. I was committed to Naomi and our life together. My work still took up most of my time but coming home to Naomi seemed to make it all worthwhile.

I met Alf, the manager of Oasis (which was run by the Salvation Army) at an open day at Odyssey House. He was an interesting character and he asked me about my job at YSAS and whether I was interested in working in the areas of mental health and drug and alcohol. I had become frustrated with some of the staff and procedures at YSAS and before I knew it, I had agreed to begin working at Oasis as a support worker with dual diagnosed clients, those with a mental illness and substance abuse problem.

Some of the people I supported at Oasis had very complex conditions from personality disorders, schizophrenia, bipolar disorder, major depression and brain damage, and were also addicted to drugs and alcohol. My clients needed support with basic living skills such as hygiene, nutrition and medication, as well as more complex issues such as looming court cases. I often had to visit mental health institutions and spend many hours with very lonely and troubled clients. I was supporting up to eight people at a time, both male and females.

At the time, mental health organisations wouldn't treat some people with drug and alcohol problems until they were clean, and drug and alcohol agencies were not equipped to manage mentally ill patients. Most therefore ended up in prison, would commit suicide or die of a drug overdose. While I was working at Oasis, a couple of clients were also shot by police in the streets. During one particularly difficult time, Oasis lost eight clients in a matter of 10 months.

Despite the difficulties, I enjoyed the work and during my time there Oasis was recognised with national awards for achievement in developing and implementing an innovative intensive support network in the community. However, it was demanding work, and combined with the guilt of not spending enough time at home, the stress of trying to maintain a relationship with my four children and managing my own recovery, I found myself once again struggling to cope and find balance in my life.

After a while some of the other staff were also burning out. Alf left to start a new program and some staff followed him. The Salvation Army restructured Oasis and moved Bill (the psychologist) and myself to the Flagstaff crisis accommodation facility in North Melbourne.

FARM LIFE

I had been spending time at Vicki and Peter's farm at Flinders when I needed a break from the stresses of my life. It was 60 acres of the most beautiful countryside and a peaceful environment to restore calm and perspective. Occasionally I would take a client with me and we would contribute by doing some work on the land.

After years working in city streets and in offices, working outside on the land felt like the best thing that had ever happened to me.

I wasn't happy with my new role at Flagstaff so after discussions with Vicki and Peter I decided to leave and work for myself, managing their farm with the help of some of the substance abuse clients at Salvation Army who needed time away from the streets and ongoing support.

Most of the people I brought to Flinders had never been anywhere so beautiful in all their lives. Some had never left the city. The look on their faces as we drove to the farm was priceless. The calming effect of the natural environment was immediate.

Each morning we drove an hour to the Peninsula, arriving about 8am. The work was varied and included mowing lawns, weeding, planting trees, mulching, pruning, building fences, taking care of the vegetable garden and watering the fruit trees.

I had met Vicki many years earlier at the Lighthouse Foundation and she had been a mentor to me, always encouraging and supporting me. We enjoyed a trust that I had not experienced before. Peter was a landscape designer and was able to teach me - and some of the people I brought with me – new skills and interesting knowledge about growing and harvesting fruit and other produce.

When Vicki and Peter built a two-bedroom bunkhouse in the bottom paddock I was sometimes able to stay overnight with some of the clients. After a good day's work, we'd ride around on the tractors looking at the wetlands and then I would light a little fire, cook some amazing barbecues and watch the stars. When listening closely we could also hear the sea across the hills.

Most of the drug and alcohol clients responded well to the opportunity to get away, do a little work, and then chill under the stars. However, some of my clients had significant mental health problems and were at times more difficult to support. One of my first complex clients, Matty, was a good worker but some days he was still intoxicated from the night before and was taking prescribed medication. Some mornings when I picked him up from Flagstaff I would have to carry him to the car. He would sleep during the drive and only once we were at Flinders would he wake up and contribute to the day's work.

At times there was a conflict between taking care of the farm and taking care of the people I was working with. Occasionally Vicki would have to step in to help resolve an issue but, overall, managing the farm was a positive and valuable experience for us all.

Over several years, I took more than 100 people to the farm to work, to relax, for peace and quiet, to have some time away from the city. The farm became a true sanctuary for me and many, many others.

Life was good. Being clean again, seeing all four of my kids regularly, working on the farm, and enjoying a healthy relationship with Naomi was everything I wanted; I felt like the luckiest man alive. Our plan was progressing well – we were into our third year.

GIOVANNI OTTONE

Dad passed away at the Austin Hospital on 27 July 2000 from pancreatic cancer. He had been in hospital for two and a half weeks and I had visited him almost daily. I would say hello and not much else as his English was poor and I spoke very little Italian. Mostly I would sit beside him and he would sometimes moan as the pain got worse.

One day he asked me to rub some cream into his face which was very dry. A tear ran down my face as I rubbed in the cream and realised that I had really never touched my dad before. I continued to rub his face long after the cream was absorbed; I didn't want to stop as I knew I would probably never touch him again. It was a special moment.

When I received the phone call on the morning my dad passed I felt grateful that as much as I had disappointed him throughout my life, Dad had lived long enough to finally see me doing well, sober and clean with a good job, a relationship and my kids in my life.

The family gathered around his bed to pay their respects and say goodbye. Sam made the first move, walking up to him to say a few words and kissing him before walking out. I followed but really I had already said goodbye the day I had rubbed cream into his face.

My father had never given me loving advice; during most of my younger years he was under the influence of alcohol and intimidating, often in a rage and frequently putting me down. Growing up, I hated my father. For most of my life I had felt his shame and embarrassment that I had failed him as a son: I was a drug addict, in and out of jail, a lost soul. He never really said much to me but I could feel the disgust when he looked at me.

Giovanni Ottone had loved a drink but he had also been a really hard worker his whole life; he put food on the table and he loved his kids in his way. He tried hard to do the right thing; he took me with him to work when I started getting into trouble thinking that would help, and at times he gave me money. He tried to discipline me with his beatings - he was loving me the only way he knew how.

I made peace with my dad. I'm glad he didn't see me further destroy what I had achieved; it would have been no surprise to him that my struggle with addiction was not over.

ITALY

Mum had spent her life caring for everyone but herself: cooking, cleaning, washing, supporting her family. For someone who had never gone to school, she managed the best she could, putting up with my dad and 10 children. In my eyes she was the mother of the century. I had always wanted to visit the village where I was born so I decided to surprise her by turning up in Italy while she was there visiting family. The timing was good, I had been working hard and had a few weeks holiday owing.

It was a long flight; I missed Naomi and was disappointed to be missing the end of the football season as the Brisbane Lions, the team I had supported all my life, had finally made it to a grand final. I reminded myself that I was making the journey for my mum, as much as for me.

Although I had wanted to surprise Mum, I decided at the last minute to let her know that I was coming and arranged to meet her, and a cousin I had never met, at the airport in Milan. They were very happy to see me and a lot of Italian was spoken. I could make out most of what was said but couldn't respond fluently, so I nodded and smiled a lot.

While staying in Milan with our relatives I managed to attend a couple of meetings of Narcotics Anonymous and Alcoholics Anonymous.

After a week we took a seven-hour train trip to Potenza in southern Italy. The train was packed so I made the ride as comfortable as I could for Mum, using luggage to construct her a seat, while I stood over her the whole way. People were sleeping on the floor and there was no room to do anything. We finally arrived at 7am and one of my many cousins met us and drove us for an hour to Corleto, the village where Mum was born.

We were greeted by our large Italian family including Mum's sisters, nieces and nephews. The hospitality was amazing; cousins I'd never met slept on floors so we could sleep in beds. The houses were tiny and the smells were unfamiliar but the food was second to none. I will never forget the feasts that were prepared for us. Everyone kept trying to get me to drink alcohol; they couldn't understand that I didn't drink. Every meal time I was offered alcohol. No thanks.

Spending time with Mum in Italy was different to anything I had experienced before. Her memory was amazing and she was able to share so much about the history of her village and our relatives in the cemetery. I was particularly interested to see the room where my siblings and I were born – it was basically a shelter for chickens, a barn.

Most of the time I was preoccupied with thoughts of home. Occasionally I'd ring up Naomi and the kids and that would brighten my day. Jason Akermanis won the Brownlow Medal while I was away and the Brisbane Lions went on to win the flag. I was over the moon with happiness.

As soon as I got home I visited the kids at school, caught up with Naomi and then sat down to watch a replay of the grand final. Go Lions!

TIYLA

One day I received a phone call from Naomi; she was crying and I couldn't make any sense of what she was saying. When she calmed down she explained that her sister Lisa was in the process of losing her child to human services because she was suffering from mental health and other significant issues.

I suggested that we offer to take the child into our own care; we discussed it briefly and decided it was something we could manage. It was to be a temporary situation until her permanent care could be sorted out.

I will never forget the day Tiyla came into our lives. I felt I had failed as a father in the past and by taking Tiyla into our care and keeping her out of the foster system, I had an opportunity to do the right thing. It's a decision I have never regretted.

As great as it was to have Tiyla, we had no idea of the pressures of caring for a young child. Initially she was not in a good way, undernourished and a very frightened little angel. Tiyla warmed to Naomi immediately, however it took hard work and patience before she felt close to me.

In the following years her parents fought to get Tiyla back and we were involved in a number of court cases to determine custody. However both her mum and dad were using drugs and leading chaotic lives and were granted only supervised visits.

I started to feel the pressures in my life gather momentum but for a while I was able to manage the stress. Working with mentally ill people was challenging, and coping with the care and custody issues of Tiyla was demanding; sometimes life felt overwhelming.

I started to hang around with some of the shady characters that I met during my visits to prison and who would tempt me with offers of drugs and money. When my life was tracking well I found it easy to resist. But under stress I convinced myself that it was fine to accept just a little money, a small amount of drugs. Gradually I got sucked back into old habits.

Naomi was taking care of Tiyla, the house, and at times me when I was spending too much time working, attending meetings and hanging around with people I should have stayed away from.

Tiyla had been with us for over a year when Naomi became pregnant; sadly, the pregnancy ended in a miscarriage and she ended up in hospital. We were in the process of planning our wedding at the time and it was very traumatic for Naomi. I didn't really understand what she was going through but tried to be supportive.

THE WEDDING

On 4 October 2003 Naomi and I got married in Flinders. The celebrations took place at the beautiful farm owned by Vicki and Peter where I was still working. The day was so special and helped put some of our struggles into perspective.

The night before I got married, my brother Rob, who was the best man, and my son Dean stayed over. Rob suggested that we celebrate with a drink. I knew it was not a good idea but I was nervous about the wedding and I found myself agreeing. After four years of being clean and sober I picked the eve of the most special day of my life to have a drink.

The wedding day was surreal; I was marrying the most beautiful woman in the world, surrounded by my favorite people at my favorite place in the world. Most of my family were present and Vicki and Peter were there as usual to offer their unconditional support. Naomi's dad and my brother Rob gave speeches that brought tears to my eyes. It really was the perfect day.

PART SEVEN – RELAPSE
2003 – 2008

THE HONEYMOON IS OVER

Our wedding day ended late afternoon and we returned to Melbourne to stay at Crown for a couple of nights before our honeymoon to Thailand. Naomi was still recovering from the miscarriage; she was exhausted and wanted to go to bed so I took the opportunity to go out drinking for most of the night. I continued to drink for the next few weeks in Thailand, all the time kidding myself that I would be okay.

When we got back from the honeymoon, I stopped going to meetings because I was still drinking. Naomi was not conscious of my addiction patterns and initially, thought little of it. Occasionally I would smoke a bit of dope and, soon enough, I progressed to ecstasy and speed. I had started playing hide and seek: I would hide my drug use as long as possible and live in fear of being caught.

Heroin was the only real drug for me and, within a few months, I was using again as if I had never stopped. I continued to hide the truth from Naomi and I didn't concern myself with what she was going through; I was so selfish, I made it all about me.

It was the most hectic time of my life. The house was being renovated and Naomi was pregnant again and looking after Tiyla, so we decided it would be a good idea for Naomi to move home to her mum and dad's while I slept in the garage at the back of the house. I thought I could use this time to get my act together. Instead, I continued using and even started selling drugs to fund my own habit and to maintain a lifestyle beyond our means. The renovation was expensive and I got caught up in trying to keep up

THE HONEYMOON IS OVER

the facade of success.

I was smoking dope, shooting heroin and popping pills. The dope was making me paranoid so I borrowed a gun from a friend and slept with it under my pillow. Then, I would attempt to pull up for a while and to help Naomi with the house and Tiyla. But I could never hold it together for long.

Jake Robert Ottone was born on the 14 August 2004. The night he was born Naomi was rushed into surgery after many hours of labour and I was left holding my son. I started crying and promised myself that I would stop fucking around and do the right thing. It was a promise I wasn't able to keep. Responsibility had always felt too heavy for me.

CHAOS

Home was my only link to sanity. Coming home to my wife, my children, my house, my dog, my car, provided me with the stability I needed. But when I woke up to go to work, my mind was in chaos. I would wake wondering what I should use to get through the day.

Despite the fact that I was using again, I kept working at Flagstaff two days a week and at the farm three days a week. I was working with complex needs clients including Matty who was using and difficult to manage; Chris who had spent most of his life in prison and was on heaps of methadone; and Cutcha who had also been in prison, had a major personality disorder and was out of control on ice, paranoid and at times psychotic. I was leading a double life and avoiding the reality that I wasn't strong enough to help anyone.

We didn't stay overnight at the farm often as the guys had to be in town for appointments, medication and reporting. So most days I would pick them all up and drive them to Flinders myself. One particular morning I collected Chris and Matty from Yarraville where they lived together, then went to pick up Cutcha in West Footscray. He seemed a little odd - listening to head banging music and agitated - but assured me he was okay. Once we got to the farm we planned the jobs for the day and set about our work. Matty and Cutcha were niggling each other and Chris was trying to keep the peace.

However the drama escalated when Cutcha, who had been up for days without sleep after using copious amounts of ice, started having a psychotic episode. He called Matty a dog and threatened to bash him, so Matty was freaking out. Chris wanted to sort things out the prison way by hitting Cutcha over the head.

The situation was spiralling out of control. I tried to call the staff at Flagstaff but no one answered the phone. I wanted to leave but Cutcha wouldn't stop mowing the lawn; he just kept mowing up and down the aisle between the hazelnuts obsessively. We basically had to wait for the mower to run out of petrol before he would stop. He was ranting and raving about what he was going to do to Matty – he really wanted to kill him. Chris wanted to bash both Cutcha and Matty. Well, the scene was fucking crazy and the staff from Flagstaff weren't calling me back.

I separated Matty and Cutcha and was also able to calm Chris down so that he could help me if the violence between Cutcha and Matty escalated. We managed to pack up the farm and get into the car. I told Cutcha to get in the front passenger side and told Matty and Chris to get in the back. The drive back to Melbourne was intense! Cutcha continued to make serious threats, Matty was clearly petrified and Chris was on edge.

On the outskirts of Melbourne I suggested that Matty get out of the car and catch a train the rest of the way home. He agreed but said he couldn't walk the streets with this on him, and from his pants he pulled a huge machete which he had taken from the farm and that he claimed to be carrying for his own protection.

Somehow, I was able to retrieve the machete from Matty, give him $20 and drop him at the train station. I still hadn't heard back from Flagstaff and was in a state of panic. Cutcha noticed the machete and again started ranting and raving, threatening to use it on me; Chris was ready to pounce if he had to.

I managed to calm Cutcha down for a few minutes by allowing him to smoke in the car. The staff from Flagstaff finally called back – they had been in hospital with another client of mine and were deciding whether to turn off his life support. I couldn't really talk but said I would come in after I dropped the boys off.

After taking Chris home I was able to calm Cutcha down surprisingly easily with an offer of $30; he forgot about his threats and was distracted for the rest of the drive. When I dropped him home he even asked me what time I was picking him up in the morning and I realised he had no real understanding about the chaos he had created that day.

When I arrived back at Flagstaff the staff were sitting around having cups of tea. I asked Bill the psychologist if I could see him in his office and as soon as we walked in I fell apart with rage as I relayed the days' events. He apologised on behalf of the staff and I was able to vent for a while but I was in no shape to go home to Naomi and the kids. I was in a state and wasn't coping at all. Bill and I decided to get together again in the morning to continue the discussion and write an incident report.

I was told not to work with Cutcha for a while, but the following day he had an appointment with his parole officer and I was the only one available to take him. So stupidly I again got stuck with him and again had to deal with his aggressive, paranoid and psychotic behavior. He threatened to kill his parole officer and again threatened to kill Matty.

I hadn't recovered from the machete incident from the day before. I'd had enough and went back to work and spoke to Bill again at length. I filed an incident report and went to see a doctor who gave me a certificate to excuse me from work until I had my stress under control.

However the staff at Flagstaff found out that I had been using and the doctor's certificate was rejected. I was given an opportunity to resign and offered six weeks' pay. That day I gave up all my attempts to hold it together and completely lost the plot.

DENIAL (DON'T EVEN KNOW I AM LYING)

Naomi and I were not getting along; she despised my using and couldn't cope with my lifestyle so I started to stay in Flinders.

Staying at the farm should have been a great opportunity to get clean and pull myself together, but controlling my drug use was not something I could ever manage on my own. Heroin was the perfect painkiller for me, the perfect drug to quieten my mind and numb my emotional anguish. No other drug could do for me what heroin could.

Jack, a friend who had been living in Thailand, came back to Melbourne with some (apparently) pure heroin and I was off again. Vicki and Peter had trusted me and I put our friendship at risk.

Christmas 2005 and New Years were a disaster; Naomi was barely holding it together with the support of her family and friends and my two eldest daughters. We agreed that I would stay away until I got clean, however, at every opportunity I would drive to Melbourne to score drugs. This became my life: living at the farm, scoring drugs, and attempting to do farm work while I was using.

Vicki and Peter went overseas and I started feeling guilty about using at the farm so Jack and I decided to get a motel room in Flinders. At that point, our using totally escalated. We were buying massive amounts of drugs for ourselves and scoring for other people and we always ended up back at the motel to get stoned.

At the beginning of 2006 my using was the worst it had ever been. In the past when I had used I was looking for relief and a rush

DENIAL (DON'T EVEN KNOW I AM LYING)

of wellbeing, a short period of escape. This time I was dealing with being unemployed and the pain of separating from Naomi and the kids, and my using became obsessive and chaotic. I was using copious amounts of heroin to numb everything, then I'd use speed, ecstasy, cocaine. I'd never used like this before. I felt like life had no purpose and I wanted to die. I was looking for oblivion.

CATCH ME IF YOU CAN

At the end of March, we decided to leave the motel in Flinders and book into a motel in the city. After a couple of nights I went to see Naomi; I had lost weight and looked like shit and when she saw me she started to cry. Naomi didn't want me around the kids until I was clean and so I left.

One day, Jack's friend Tania asked us to buy her some cocaine. We all put in and Jack and I went to the Docklands, where I knew a guy who was selling drugs, and we bought an ounce of coke for $8000. A quarter was for Tania, and Jack and I went halves in the rest. I also purchased a large quantity of ecstasy tablets; I don't know why I got so much, I already had heroin and speed on me. We booked into The Como Hotel in South Yarra and for the next three days we used most of the cocaine. By that stage Jack started flipping out and becoming psychotic, walking up and down the hallway thinking the place was surrounded by cops. Tania tried to contain him but then I flipped out too, paranoid that the cops were going to be called.

I gathered my belongings including all the evidence – syringes, drugs, money and empty bottles of alcohol – and took off in the car we had hired; I didn't know where I was going but I had to get out of there.

I had been using cocaine, heroin and amphetamines for three days and I hadn't slept or had anything to eat. I didn't know what I was doing, I was just driving around – I really don't know how; I had a death wish. I felt totally screwed like I was revisiting hell.

That day I visited my mum, two of my closest friends and my psychologist; I think I was saying goodbye, I wanted out. My mum was distraught to see me in that state after I had been well for so many years. My friends tried to take my keys and my psych didn't know what to do. After leaving each house I would pull over to have some coke, a stimulant, then heroin to come down, followed by speed to wake me up from being on the nod. Fucking totally insane.

I got a call from Nicky. He wanted to score so I arranged to meet him at the pub across the road from my brother Sam's house. My brother couldn't believe the state I was in and also tried to take the car keys. I left his place to meet Nicky, gave him his drugs and left at about 11pm. I kept driving, then stopping to use and driving some more. I started praying like I'd never prayed before. Please god, if you're there, fucking help.

Somehow I made it to West Footscray. I wanted so much to see Naomi, Tiyla and Jake and maybe ask for help, but I couldn't bring myself to knock on the door. Was this rock bottom? Around 1am, I was parked on Roberts Street just down the road from our house. I had another taste and took off, still praying for help.

As I pulled up at the lights at Geelong Road, a cop car pulled up in front of me with its lights flashing. I was so stoned I didn't know what was going on. The cops told me to get out of the car but I couldn't, my legs kept hitting the panel. The cops had to help me get out and stand me up against the fence. They thought I was drunk but after a breathalyser they realised that I was catatonic. Another cop car pulled up. I had no energy to run, no fight left. Were my prayers being answered? The cops had no idea what was about to unfold and I was in no state to care or do anything about it.

They started searching the car – bingo! The cops found a bag full of ecstasy pills, what was left of the coke, some rocks of heroin, syringes and a bag full of money – just under $20,000. The handcuffs went on and I was put in the police car while the search continued. My life flashed before me, my past back to haunt me. All the hard work I had done was gone, the awards I had received were useless, my children were a memory, my wife a dream.

I was taken to the police station in Footscray and placed in a room. I can remember literally bouncing off the walls. My using had finally been stopped, it was over. My prayers had been answered by men in blue uniform. Fuck!

APRIL FOOL

I was very stoned but I recall that detectives kept coming in and attempting to talk to me, then leaving. They accused me of being a drug lord, running a syndicate, dealing and more. Really, I was just a desperate junkie, only barely alive. With the amount of drugs in my system it was going to take days for me to come down.

I was questioned all night long. At some point I was charged with trafficking a commercial quantity of drugs, and use and possession of drugs of dependence. Trafficking and proceeds of crime - in other words I was fucked.

I was handcuffed and driven to my home in a procession of six police cars that included the dog squad, the drug squad and arresting detectives. Having found so many drugs in the car, they expected to find a huge quantity at my house. I was still suffering the effects of the drugs in my system and at times needed support just to stand up.

I will never forget the feeling of shame when Naomi answered the knock at the door with our baby Jake in her arms. Immediately she started crying as the police introduced themselves and explained that they were there to search the premises.

I was taken into the house and made to sit on the lounge. Cops everywhere. Naomi and I both knew there was nothing in the house but we also understood the process. I asked Naomi if I could hug Jake. She said no and asked the cops if she could leave while they continued their search.

COMING CLEAN

I was fucking angry. I was handcuffed, not allowed to hug my son, still feeling the effects of the drugs, and heavily charged. My wife, who I really loved, had walked out with my son. I was more alone than I had ever felt and I had no one to blame but myself.

The police spent a few hours conducting a thorough search but found nothing. I was taken back to the police station where I was finally seen by a doctor; he was concerned about my condition and gave me some medication to help me calm down.

I was finally taken to the cells at the Sunshine police station and processed. I hadn't been to jail for nearly 20 years and most of that time I'd been clean and sober. But when I fell off I really fell off – there were no half measures for me.

My time in the cells really was the foot up the arse I had needed. I spent most of the time lying on my bed totally exhausted, detoxing from all the drugs in my system. I slept for the first four days and when I started to come around I felt so embarrassed and ashamed I just wanted to die. My life had turned to shit and it was all my own fault.

The cells were the same as they had been 20 years previously – overcrowded, food unfit for animals, crims glorifying their crimes, scamming, drugs, and the occasional inmate who genuinely wanted a second chance.

Naomi came to see me; it wasn't pleasant. She was upset and angry and told me that if I used again she was walking. For the first time I didn't have anything to say; I was guilty and the shame was overwhelming.

After 12 days on remand at the Sunshine police station I was transferred to the court house for my bail application. The magistrate took into account my attempts at recovery and the good work I had done in the community. I was given bail with the strict conditions that I report three times a week to the Footscray police station, report to a psychiatrist to treat my mental health issues, admit myself to the Victorian Addiction Centre for 28 days and abstain from all mood and mind-altering drugs.

I had a lot of support in the courtroom from my family, some of my children, friends and co-workers. Naomi was there and Vicki and Peter had flown all the way from Los Angeles to show their support. Why I continued to feel unloved is beyond me.

BAILED

Before checking in to the Victorian Addiction Centre I had the opportunity to spend some time with Tiyla, Jake and Naomi which made me realise just how lucky and blessed I was, and how stupid I had been to risk losing my family. What was fucking wrong with me?

My children Michaela, Dean, Chantelle and Teryn were all very happy I had been given bail and were praying for me. My mother and some of my siblings were also praying that I would recover from this relapse and would get my life back on track.

I booked into the addiction centre in Ivanhoe; it was the first time I had been to a private rehab clinic as I now had private health cover. It was a very humbling experience. I had been in and out of recovery since 1989 and most of that time I had been clean and sober and working in the field supporting others. I was no longer the guru I thought I was, no longer the mentor - I had certainly fallen off the pedestal. It was harder than I had expected. I had to take the cotton wool out of my ears and shove it into my mouth so that I would listen up and listen good.

I was challenged, confronted and exposed. I could no longer hide behind the work I had done helping others and, after a couple of weeks, I could admit that I was full of shit and that I needed to surrender to the process. My schedule included a daily walk, meetings on issues such as relapse prevention, anger management and nutrition, as well as counselling. We were also taken to regular meetings of AA and NA.

BAILED

It was a fortnight before my first visit. Naomi, Tiyla and Jake all came to see me. The hugs and kisses from the kids made my day, however, understandably, Naomi was a little reserved and cold. My brothers Sam and Robert also came to see me and seemed to really care about how I was going.

After four weeks I was ready to go home; the rehab had really helped and had given me the opportunity to reflect. I knew that I had been given another chance. I was on bail for very serious charges and there was a good chance I would go to jail for a long time, so it was all up to me.

The hard work began: reporting three times a week at the addiction centre, attending meetings, and doing my best at home with Naomi and the kids. Looking after myself had never been a priority, but I was starting to learn that I was unable to live a healthy and balanced life if I didn't take care of myself.

Things between Naomi and me had changed; I had put her through too much pain and the connection and trust between us was gone. The house, our vehicles and bank accounts were all frozen which infuriated Naomi and strained our relationship even further. She was very angry about the position we were in: having to find a solicitor, attend committal hearings, adjournments. The case was expected to go ahead in 2007 and I was advised to take it to trial and plead not guilty.

One morning at a cafe in Yarraville, Naomi dropped the bomb – she'd had enough and wanted out of the relationship. I could not believe it. Naomi had had plenty of opportunities to leave; I had even asked her while I was in rehab if she wanted to leave. She had answered that as long as I didn't use again she was going to hang on.

COMING CLEAN

I had known Naomi was barely managing, but that hadn't prepared me at all. I was absolutely devastated, broken, defeated. A week later Naomi and the kids moved into a house in Kingsville. As Naomi said on her way out, this was karma.

The shock of Naomi and the kids leaving affected me like never before, partly because I was clean and not numbing myself with drugs. Feelings that I had suppressed for so long started to surface.

Counselling, after care at the addiction centre, meetings of NA and AA, and the support of some family members and close friends kept me sane. At times, I really didn't want to go on but somehow I found the courage and strength to get through.

My psychiatrist was treating me for post-traumatic stress disorder and after some months I was able to respond and slowly began to feel better, although the pain of losing my family continued to linger.

After nine months I was surprised but pleased to be offered a job at the Victorian Addiction Centre. I knew that working in the drug and alcohol field had contributed to my relapse but I thought that it might help my court case to have stable employment at the addiction centre that the court had bailed me to. It hadn't been part of my plan but I took the job.

I began to meditate every day and completed a course in mindfulness. Meditation and mindfulness provided me with calmness and contentment, and the ability to carefully consider my choices. This in turn helped me to stop smoking, eat well and take better care of myself.

I was 48 years old and my life was finally falling into place; I was reconnecting with my children, and making some good friends.

BAILED

However my pending court case was hanging over my head, I was reporting three times a week to the Footscray police station, and the possibility of going to jail was real.

I had been clean and sober for more than two years and was working at the addiction centre. When my trial date was set, I felt ready to face the consequences of my last relapse.

THE TRIAL

After two years of waiting, it was finally time for my case to go to trial. My barrister was Peter Morrissey and he worked with solicitor Matthew White. They were both very professional and took the work seriously.

The job of the prosecution was to prove my guilt, which didn't seem too difficult considering the evidence: the drugs, paraphernalia, and money; the room at The Como and the scene with Jack and Tania in the hallway; and the hire car. However, my lawyers argued that the police had withheld evidence, as they had sworn under oath that no wallet had been found in the car, which contradicted the property book which recorded that Jack's wallet had been found. This created doubt about the prosecution's case and strengthened the argument that the drugs, like the wallet, could also have belonged to someone else.

The fear of being found guilty was very real and the longer the trial lasted, the more I agonised about a guilty verdict. I'd lost everything: my wife, children, respect … and now I was about to lose my freedom.

Once all the evidence was heard, the judge explained the four charges to the jury:

1. Trafficking a commercial quantity of drug of dependence
2. Trafficking a drug of dependence
3. Proceeds of crime money
4. Possession and use of a drug of dependence

THE TRIAL

Having been on trial before, I knew that waiting for the verdict would be excruciating. We waited for a couple of hours with no word from the jury, which I was convinced was a bad sign for me. The barrister spoke to me for a while, telling me we'd done our best and it was out of our hands.

Finally it was time to hear the verdict and everyone filed back into court. There were no reporters which was good, but my brothers Sam and Robert, my sister Marie, and her husband Ray were there with a couple of friends and everyone appeared nervous.

I sat in the dock at the back of the court; the barristers and the prosecution were all in their place along the main bench. We heard the infamous knock on the door and the order from the court official, "All stand".

The presiding judge walked in and told us to all sit before inviting the jury in. As they filed in, I felt a surrender I had never experienced before; the fight was over and I was ready for the result. I closed my eyes and waited.

"Has the jury reached a verdict? How does the jury find the defendant on the charges?"

"We, the jury find the defendant Leonard John Ottone not guilty on charges one, two and three. We, the jury find Leonard John Ottone guilty on charge four - guilty of possession and use of a drug of dependence."

I was charged a total of $3000 and released to the hugs and tears of relieved family and friends. The judge congratulated me for doing an amazing job of rehabilitating myself and encouraged me to do something with this special opportunity. I looked up in a silent prayer of thanks.

PART EIGHT - MOVING ON
2009 - 2016

FRESH START

The court case was over. I was no longer required to report to the police, and the assets that had been frozen were returned to me, including the house, both our cars and the $18,000 found on me the night I was arrested. However the trial had been very painful emotionally. And strangely, while I managed well while the case was hanging over my head, I seemed to struggle more once it was over.

Naomi started court proceedings to determine custody of our children and a financial settlement. A long and difficult chapter of blaming and finger pointing followed as neither of us were prepared to compromise. It was supposed to be about the kids but in the end the issues were resolved with money. Naomi finally agreed to a settlement which meant I had to either get a loan or sell the house to pay her out. At first I hoped to manage with a loan but it soon became clear that I would have to sell the house.

Naomi was given custody of the children – Tiyla was about six and Jake was two years old – while I had access every second weekend and on Wednesdays after school. I wrestled with dark thoughts, self-doubt, feelings of failure. What was the fucking point? Three years had passed since my last relapse and I was still dealing with the destruction I had created.

Thankfully, I got through the hard times with the support of family and close friends, the love I had from all of my kids, the constant prayers of my mum, and by continuing to attend meetings.

Selling the house didn't take long as it was located in a sought-after area. I gave away most of everything I owned including furniture and clothes and moved in with a friend, Vince in an apartment in St Kilda Road, South Yarra. I was no longer enjoying my work and I decided it was a good time to leave and focus on looking after myself. The Victorian Addiction Centre had served its purpose and it was time for a change.

I was clean and sober, the court case was behind me, the house was sold and my debts were paid off. I had no job or relationship to distract me and I was gradually learning to live with myself, which was very difficult for me but I carried on. It felt like a good opportunity to make some other positive changes in my life.

My general practitioner, Dr John Chow suggested that I begin a course of treatment for hepatitis C. It seemed like an appropriate time so I started the treatment: an interferon injection once a week, followed by tablets daily.

In 1989, at Pleasant View I had been given a series of blood tests. I was called into the office and told there was good news and bad news: the good news was I didn't have AIDS but the bad news was I had contracted hepatitis C. At the time the news meant little to me. I knew it was a virus in the blood and I knew I had probably contracted it in prison from sharing filthy needles. We would sharpen the needles on concrete floors or on the sides of old matchboxes and pass them around hundreds of times. At times, the syringes were so blunt I needed to stab myself to get the needle into my arm. I could also have contracted the virus from the needles other prisoners had used when giving me tattoos, or the old razor blades we used for shaving that were also shared.

After I got out of jail I continued to share needles. For desperate users like me, finding a clean needle before a fix is the last thing on your mind. I haven't come across too many users who refuse to share needles for fear of contracting blood borne diseases.

The side effects of the interferon were horrific: aching bones, no energy, no appetite, cold-like symptoms. My skin turned grey and I spent most of my time lying down. A session in the sauna and spa (on the same floor as the apartment) seemed to help if I could make it there, but more than that was a huge effort.

I forced myself to continue to have the kids on the weekends but I couldn't do much with them. I also attended meetings where people like myself had been through the same treatment and understood what I was going through.

The treatment was another reminder of the consequences of the unsafe practices of my past. I hadn't been concerned about hepatitis C when I was using, however once I was clean I had to start looking after my health - treating the hepatitis, getting my teeth fixed and seeking professional help. It was all part of looking after myself, which I had never done before.

The interferon treatment lasted six months, however the relentless pain continued after I completed the course of medication. I was really looking forward to my final blood test and confirming that I was cleared of hepatitis C. However the doctor gave me the bad news that the treatment had failed and the virus could still be detected in my system. He told me that new medications were being trialled with a higher success rate but this didn't make me feel better at all.

I was so angry that I had spent six months going through hell for nothing. It was difficult to accept but I knew that I had to move on. It took a while but I slowly started to get my energy back, returned to training and physically felt much better.

I was also really enjoying the time I spent with my kids. Jake and Tiyla in particular loved to come to the apartment to hang out in the pool and spa and then go out to eat. I attended meetings consistently, sought the support I needed and found it easier to look after myself. I started to feel like life was worth living.

I spoke to an employment agency and was encouraged to go back to school to undertake a full-time diploma in community services with counselling, drug and alcohol, and mental health components.

I enrolled in a course at Prahran TAFE in High Street, Prahran, a short distance from where I was living. The thought of returning to school scared the hell out of me and I nearly talked myself out of going. Somehow I managed to put my self-doubt behind me and attend the course.

I was totally out of my comfort zone as a mature aged student. However, my friends reminded me how far I had come: I had been uneducated, institutionalised, drug addicted, homeless, mentally ill. To come back from that was a miracle and mistakes were bound to happen but the fact that I had always picked myself up and soldiered on was a strength that had given many people hope. I also strongly believed I had to do something worthwhile and so I continued with the course.

I wanted desperately to learn, however with my personal experiences, I sometimes found it difficult to listen to some of the statements of the facilitators, for example the claim that drug and alcohol addictions were a choice. This comment angered and frustrated me however I made every effort to bite my tongue and only express my opinions at appropriate moments. At times I wrote my thoughts in assignments.

I connected with a few of my peers who offered support and guidance. In particular, another student Rob, who was my age and had expertise in the legal system, helped me immensely. I did the best I could with assignments and projects and friends helped with typing and using computers.

I completed the course in 2012 and was both excited and proud that I had achieved something that had seemed impossible, in spite of the voice in my head constantly telling me that I failed at everything and should just give up.

With school complete, I decided to follow my dream to set up my own not-for-profit organisation for the care and resettlement of drug users seeking recovery.

VICDOR

In 2012, I established the Vicdor Living Centre with the support of family, friends and some valued colleagues. The process was long and hard and when I started I had no idea what was involved. Just to register as a not-for-profit organisation was complex and time consuming. However I had heaps of energy and went to work.

My sister Marie and her husband Ray had a property in Wallan, Victoria - five acres of beautiful countryside where I had previously taken some people who needed to stay in a safe environment while waiting for a place in long-term rehabilitation.

I had the idea that the property would be a great setting to establish a rehabilitation centre, so I met with my sister and Ray to discuss the possibilities. They supported me from the beginning and offered the use of the property rent free for three months.

Suddenly it seemed that my plan was achievable. I still had my doubts and I totally understood that with all of my past mistakes I would have obstacles to overcome. Some people would not trust me and others would doubt my judgement. However, I had a great team supporting me. The board was outstanding, Vicki was the patron and I was the live-in CEO. Many fantastic volunteers supported the initiative and travelled long distances to help out with cooking, facilitating groups and occasionally sleeping over to give me a break.

Finally, we were ready to open. The centre attracted participants straight away with no need for advertising. Fees were set for those who could afford them and I negotiated a small contribution for those who couldn't. For patients with no money at all, I would try to find someone to sponsor them or provide a charity bed in exchange for small jobs around the facility.

On 4 October 2012 we held a Vicdor Open Day which was very well attended. Vicki and Peter, Bernie Geary, Victoria's child safety commissioner, the board, volunteers and participants were all there. As part of the event I did a radio interview with 774 Melbourne about the services we offered and the funds needed to fully run a facility that was providing an essential service to the community.

The facility grew and before I knew it, the costs had blown out. At times there were more charity beds than paying beds. We were managing, but problems started to emerge and running the centre became quite stressful. Unfortunately we had limited funds to pay wages and our volunteers were gradually employed by other agencies, until I was left running the facility largely on my own.

TRAVEL

I needed a break so in August 2013 I arranged extra help at Vicdor and I went overseas with my close friend Chris. The plan was to spend three weeks traveling through London, Amsterdam and Rome with a stop on the way back in Thailand.

In London we trained physically and meditated every day and also attended a couple of meetings of NA. The highlight was to meet up with my kids, Michaela, who had taken a year off at the age of 20 to explore the world on her own, and Dean, 22, who was travelling with friends. I was so proud of my amazing children and full of love. We met up in a Turkish bar and laughed, told stories and discussed travel plans. It was a wonderful reminder of the importance of family.

I gave Dean my blessings for the rest of his trip, knowing he was travelling to have a good time and that meant getting trashed. So I asked him to be careful and to make sure his mates all looked after each other. The response was priceless: "Dad, I won't do anything you haven't already done." Ha ha!

I knew that Michaela wasn't drinking but I also worried about her travelling alone. All I could do was give her the biggest, warmest hug and then put her in a cab and watch her drive away.

We moved onto Amsterdam, a city I had wanted to visit most of my life - but for all the wrong reasons. We immediately fell in love with the city, the people, the canals and bicycles everywhere; the whole vibe of Amsterdam was great.

Chris and I were asked daily if we were looking for Charlie

TRAVEL

(cocaine). No thanks. We would look at each other, smile and move on. The night life was insane – people drinking, smoking dope, high on coke or heroin. Chris and I however behaved, did some tours, ate well and took care of each other. Attending NA meetings in Amsterdam – where drugs are treated differently than most other cities – was also an experience.

After Amsterdam we flew to Rome, an historic city full of beautiful buildings, people and food. Being able to speak and understand some Italian was helpful and the sightseeing was absolutely amazing.

I was feeling more content than I had in a very long time. This was the life I had dreamed of. I remembered the list I had written in group therapy many years ago which described the life I wanted and which inspired my first serious attempt to get clean.

I was now, at this moment, actually living that life: travelling, working for myself, living in a great place, driving a good car, clean and sober, and becoming the trustworthy, loyal and honest friend and family member I had always hoped to be. Those seemingly impossible aspirations had become my reality.

Our last stop was Thailand where we enjoyed tourist activities and relaxed. It was the perfect time to reflect and think about all that had happened throughout my life. The past was behind me and I had to accept that there was not a thing I could do to change it. I had to forgive, ask to be forgiven, help others and give myself the best chance to maintain the sanity I needed to soldier on.

I was picked up at the airport by a couple of friends and I was quickly filled in with everything that been happening at Vicdor while I was away. Apparently, the day I had left someone had brought drugs into the facility; a couple of people used and one was asked to leave after an assault took place. All hell broke loose, I was blamed for leaving and parents were upset. The police got involved and the board members had to take charge. These dramas, combined with a lack of funding and the large number of participants who couldn't afford to pay the fees, contributed to the inevitable decision to close the facility.

HOME

My time away had provided me with the clarity I needed to fully appreciate the importance of family and the need for me to concentrate on my health. It was time to move back to Melbourne to spend more time with my children and focus on maintaining my health and wellbeing.

In the next few months I moved some of the Vicdor residents to halfway houses, sold the house in Wallan and with the little money I had left over, purchased a cosy, three-bedroom home in the western suburbs close to my kids. In the meantime I continued to help others on a small scale, occasionally taking in someone either coming off drugs, relapsing from sobriety or needing some respite before entering long-term rehab. I also continued to go to a support group for men every Tuesday night.

The transition from being CEO of Vicdor to dole recipient was massive but learning to define myself by who I am and not what I do has been one of the hardest and most important lessons of my life.

I know that my battle with addiction will be with me forever. In early 2016, I was admitted to hospital for a serious knee operation. I was naturally concerned about the medication I would be given to cope with the pain, and the effect those drugs would have on my resolve to live a clean and sober life.

I woke from the operation groggy and spaced out from the pain killers; after years of opioid dependence, the feeling was achingly familiar. The first thing I remember was being asked if I was in pain and needed more medication. Before I could even remember to fight it, my head was nodding – yes.

For the next five days I was under the influence: morphine, Endone and other opioid-based medication. I was trying to manage the pain of the surgery but the battle raging in my mind was how to suppress the addiction that had lain dormant for 10 years.

Eventually I was allowed to go home – along with a bag of pills. For two days the drugs remained in my house while I struggled with excruciating pain in my knee. The physio told me I needed to take the medication, my doctors told me it would be fine – and my children and friends begged me not to.

On day three I started feeling the familiar effects of withdrawal, which scared the shit out of me. When my son Dean came to visit, I assured him that I hadn't taken any of the pills that remained on the bench tormenting me. Then he asked, "If you're not going to take them Dad, why are they still here?" It hit me that my addiction continued to have power over me and always would. I told Dean to flush the pills down the toilet.

One month after that operation I celebrated a decade of living without drugs and alcohol. I celebrated that milestone with the understanding that recovery is an ongoing process. One that I am facing with the love and support of family and friends.

I continue to see my psychiatrist, attend self-development courses, and attend fortnightly counselling sessions. I meditate daily, eat well and exercise regularly. In recent years, changes in government funding have led to the availability of new treatments. A few years after my first attempt, I was given another opportunity to treat the hepatitis C and this time successfully eradicated the

HOME

virus from my body.

Nurturing myself, committing to a healthy lifestyle and having faith in my recovery has made it possible for me to reconnect with my children. My relationships with my children continue to develop well. Jake, my youngest, is a joy to be with and I look forward to seeing him whenever I can. I love everything about him, especially his ability to accept me and love me. The look on his face when I pick him up is very comforting and my heart responds. Tiyla is a very special young woman to me; it makes me very proud to have her call me her dad. Her story is one that also makes me believe anything is possible. I will never be able to find the words to explain the love she has created in me.

Michaela my angel and princess has loved and supported me unconditionally. She has made me so proud with her achievements, the way she lives her life, takes risks, knows what she wants, and does what she has to do. Dino, my son, has grown into a strong young man. I don't see him as much as I would like, but whenever I do he always greets me with a hug and a kiss. I love watching him play footy, and he is always on my mind.

Recently my daughter Chantelle and my granddaughter Millie moved in with me while Chantelle resolved some difficulties at home. I have been able to listen, support and offer Chantelle and Millie a home for as long as they need. It has been an absolute pleasure to wake up in the morning to the sound of my beautiful granddaughter playing. Millie is now the same age that Chantelle was when I was at my worst and the guilt and shame and remorse I have lived with has been excruciating. So having them live with me is allowing me, in a small way, to make amends.

I am also so happy to be reconnecting with Teryn. She was so young and fragile when I hit rock bottom. I think she knew I always loved her but she felt lost in the mix. I hope I still have the opportunity to make it up to her. She has recently become a mother and I have enjoyed getting to know her little son, Maximus and spending time with them both at the park.

Ten years have passed since I last relapsed and so much has changed. The feeling of uselessness and self-pity has disappeared, my outlook on life has improved, and I intuitively know how to handle situations that used to baffle and enrage me. Some of these changes were promised to me by others who had travelled this path before me and had experienced the same miracle. I have re-established Vicdor Living Centre and continue to share the message that recovering from drug and alcohol addiction is possible.

Making mistakes is a part of life and I have made more than most. The work continues but I am committed to this way of life and I have accepted my past. I don't live there anymore.

With my mum on my wedding day. 4 October 2003

Peter Avery and Vicki Vidor. The greatest supporters ever. 2003

Representing Brosnan Youth Services. 1995

Receiving an award from Rotary Club for
services to the community. 1995

Staff at Connexions (Jesuit Social Services). 1996

Rafting on the Thompson River with Chris and Te while
working at Connexions, Jesuit Social Services. 1997

My 40th birthday. 2000
My father died soon afterwards.

With Dean and Michaela. Happier times. 2000

With Mum, visiting family in Italy. 2001

With Tiyla, an angel sent from heaven. 2002

Tiyla in Flinders at the wedding. 2003

Wtih my son Dean and my younger brother and best man, Robert. 2003

In a 1969 GS Fairmont. The car of my dreams. 2012

With Jake and Tiyla. 2005

With Jake. 2005

EPILOGUE

I was invited to a party to celebrate Vicki's 70th birthday on 27 April 2013. On the morning of the event, a voice in my head started telling me that I shouldn't go, that I didn't belong and wouldn't fit in. The mind chatter continued until I reminded myself to breathe and used my breath as an anchor. I focussed on getting ready and staying in the moment; I willed myself to go to the party and have faith that it would turn out fine.

I drove away from the farm in Wallan, stopping in front of the gate at the end of the driveway to smell the freshness of the morning. With a hint of a smile on my face and the smell of the countryside in the air, I drove down the road thinking about the day ahead.

It was a couple of hours drive to the 60-acre farm in Flinders, the most beautiful property I have ever known and a special place where I have spent much time during the highs and lows of my life. I didn't bother to turn on the radio as my mind was tuned to its own station and I reminisced about how Vicki had been one of the main people to convince me that I could succeed in my attempts at recovery. She had believed and trusted in me, had loved me when I couldn't love myself.

I had driven to the property almost daily for more than seven years while working on the land and as I got close, the memories started rushing back, particularly of my wedding there in 2003.

As I parked the car, I took a couple of deep breaths and said a few words of encouragement to myself. *Leonard, you were invited because they want you here.* I walked nervously towards the beautiful house. People were running around preparing drinks and food and well-dressed guests met each other with genuine smiles and warm words of greeting.

EPILOGUE

I spotted Vicki at the same time as she saw me. I gave her one of my best hugs, whispered happy birthday and told her how much l loved her. I was aware that everyone wanted her attention so I handed her my gifts and surrendered her to her guests.

I began to spot people I had known and who had been influential in my later life. Bill McLeod, the psychiatrist I had seen for six years while I was working at the Brosnan Centre, walked over with his wife Maggie to say hello and exchange handshakes.

My nerves slowly dissipated and I walked outside on the balcony where I was greeted by other people I had met over the years. Waiters appeared with drinks and food, and I mingled like I belonged. My past seemed to disappear into the beautiful day.

I stood on the balcony, looking out over rolling hills, trees and wetlands, down to the bottom of the paddocks where I had laboured. I recalled the people I had brought out there to rehabilitate, the good work we had done and I felt at home again.

The day had begun with self-doubt, followed by a feeling of ease and ended with me not wanting to say goodbye.

During the walk back to the car I was mindful of every step: the roll of my heel, the sensation of my toes as each foot repeated the motion. I felt the wind in my face and the satisfaction of a day fully lived.

Vicki and Peter's farm in Flinders

Back row: Me, Dean, Chantelle, Teryn, Michaela and Tiyla.
Front row: Millie (Chantelle's daughter), Jake and Max (Teryn's son). 2016

ACKNOWLEDGEMENTS

Writing this book has been a profound experience for me, helping me to confront my past and make amends for my mistakes.

The list of people I want to thank is long and includes all those who have assisted me during my many years of recovery. I hope you all know who you are and how much you mean to me. In particular I would like to express my gratitude to my family and to my six children. Without your unwavering support and guidance, I would not be here today to tell my story.

Thank you to my editors Romy Moshinsky and Georgie Raik-Allen from Real Film and Publishing. Writing has always been a challenge for me and grammar and punctuation have never been a strong point. Their valuable editorial suggestions and tireless proofreading allowed my story to be told with clarity and in my own distinct voice. I am grateful for their enthusiasm and the professionalism that they have contributed to the publication of this book. I would also like to thank Lisa Lipshut for her book design expertise.

Finally, and most importantly, I would like to express my significant gratitude to Vicki Vidor and Peter Avery for believing in me over so many years. Thank you for encouraging me to write my story and continuing to support me throughout the process.

Teryn, me holding Max, Chantelle holding Millie
and my mother Rosa. 2013

Celebrating the birthdays of Rosa and my brother, Sam with all my kids
(except Michaela who was overseas) and my granddaughter Millie. 2016

www.ingramcontent.com/pod-product-compliance
Lightning Source LLC
Chambersburg PA
CBHW020648300426
44112CB00007B/290